Copy Prep

Also from
Blueprint Publishing

The Print and Production Manual
The Print and Production Manual Practical Kit
Magazine and Journal Production
The Web Offset Directory
The Publisher's Guide Series
   Typesetting and Composition
   Interfacing Word Processors and Phototypesetters
   Desktop Publishing
   Litho Printing

Publisher's Guide Series

Copy Prep

Jill Baker

BLUEPRINT

First published in the United Kingdom 1987 by
Blueprint Publishing Ltd
Finsbury Business Centre
40 Bowling Green Lane
London EC1R 0NE
Tel 01-278 0333

British Library Cataloguing in Publication Data
Baker, Jill
   Copy prep.——(Publisher's guide series).
   1. Manuscript preparation (Authorship)
   I. Title   II. Series
   808'.02   PN160

   ISBN 0-948905-07-7

Phototypeset by Styleset Limited, Warminster, Wiltshire
Printed by Antony Rowe Ltd, Bumper's Way, Chippenham,
Wiltshire SN14 6LH

Contents

Illustrations

Acknowledgements

Despite my initial misgivings, I have enjoyed writing this book, and I should like to thank Blueprint Publishing for giving me the opportunity to do so. In the process I have borrowed where necessary from advice contained in other volumes in the Publisher's Guide Series, specifically Geoff Barlow's *Typesetting and Composition* and Michael Card's *Interfacing Word Processors and Phototypesetters*, and from *The Print and Production Manual*, ed. Peacock, Berrill and Barnard. I am also grateful to Patricia Stillwell, who made sense of an untidy manuscript, and to Kathy Smithers, for her help and advice.

JB

Introduction

I have tried in writing this book to follow my own rules. In other words, I hope it is simple and accurate and sufficiently complete for you to be able to use it to formulate answers which will work for you.

I have not attempted to write a style manual specifically for copy editors. This has already been well provided by books like Judith Butcher's *Copy Editing: The Cambridge Handbook*. My purpose has been to outline the basic disciplines across the wider range of activities involved in preparing copy for the press in the environment of a modern publishing house and I have therefore concerned myself with a combination of editorial and technical processes including such areas of current concern as coping with text on floppy discs (Chapter 4). In addition the glossary contains many of the typesetting and computer terms that editors are increasingly likely to come across.

What I have set out to do is to find answers to certain problems in such a way that the principles can be applied to other problems. In doing so I have adopted my own 'house style'; I have referred throughout to 'copy editing', though 'sub editing' is the preferred term in magazine publishing. And I have assumed that you, the readers, have too much concern for the harmony of the language to want to see the horrible 'he/she' whenever the gender of the person referred to is in doubt. And I have allowed some of my own prejudices to be apparent, as you will see.

I hope that no one will be offended by my emphasis on money. It would be disingenuous to pretend that publishing companies are in business for any reason other than to make money or that those of us who work for them, in whatever capacity, are uninterested in our own financial rewards.

Copy preparation does not enjoy the glamorous image accorded, quite mistakenly, to other areas of publishing. The scoop, the leak, the in-depth investigation, the discovery of a latter-day Dickens are not for the copy editor (nor, in truth, for many others either). Nonetheless, without the copy editor's thorough and meticulous attention, much more ill-written and inaccurate claptrap would assail the reading public, interesting and useful information would be ignored because of its presentation, and many thousands of pounds would be wasted in correcting, revising and ultimately cancelling unreadable text.

His job is vital and I hope this book will help him to do better.

1

Composition basics

Those who prepare copy for the press, be they editors or production controllers, are not normally expected to possess the skills of typographers or graphic designers, but a professional approach to the task can hardly be attempted without some knowledge of typographic terminology and some understanding of the basic principles of composition and in this chapter I have therefore attempted to cover the ground as succinctly as possible.

Terminology

Although photocomposition has superseded hot metal composition in all but a few specialist applications, the industry is still some way from accepting or agreeing any new system of terms or of typographical measurements which acknowledge this. The basis of type measurement and specification continues to be that derived from composition in metal and most of the basic terms used have been carried through intact.

Figures 1 and 2 illustrate this principle.

On the broader subject of specifying typefaces, there is frequent confusion about what constitutes a 'fount', a 'family', or a 'series'.

Founts

A fount is a complete set of sorts, all of the same typeface and point size, i.e. a complete set in one size and design of all the letters of the alphabet (upper case, small caps and lower case)

1

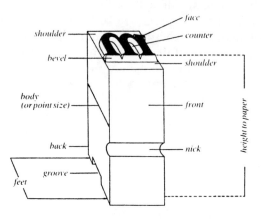

1. Parts of a metal type character

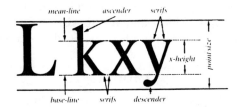

2. Terms for the printed image which derive from hot-metal composition

with associated ligatures, numerals, punctuation marks and any other signs and symbols.

In a roman fount of type (say 11pt Times, for example) there are normally three alphabets: capitals, small capitals and lower case. In an italic or bold fount of type (say 11pt Times Italic or 11pt Times Bold, for example) there are normally two alphabets: capitals and lower case.

The normal constitution of a roman (three-alphabet) fount of type is the following minimum:

Capitals: ABCDEFGHIJKLMNOPQRSTUVWXYZ
Small capitals: ABCDEFGHIJKLMNOPQRSTUVWXYZ
Lower case: abcdefghijklmnopqrstuvwxyz
Dipthongs: Æ, Œ, Æ, Œ, æ, œ

Ligatures (tied letters): ff, fi, fl, ffi, ffl
Figures: 1 2 3 4 5 6 7 8 9 0 (may be lining, non-lining, or both)
Punctuation marks: , (comma) ; (semi colon) : (colon)
. (full point) ? (question mark)
! (exclamation mark) ' (apostrophe)
- (hyphen) – (en rule) — (em rule)
Reference marks: * (asterisk) † (dagger) ‡ (double dagger)
§ (section) ‖(parallel) ¶ (paragraph)
Miscellaneous signs: () (parentheses) [] (brackets)
& (ampersand)
Accented letters (or floating accents with which to make to them):
á é í ó ú (acute)
à è ì ò ù (grave)
â ê î ô û (circumflex)
ä ë ï ö ü (diaeresis)
ç (cedilla) ñ (tilde)
Fractions: $\frac{1}{4}, \frac{1}{2}, \frac{3}{4}, \frac{1}{8}, \frac{3}{8}, \frac{5}{8}, \frac{7}{8}, \frac{1}{3}, \frac{2}{3}, \frac{1}{6}$
Mathematical signs: = × ÷ + − ′ ″ °
Commercial signs: % @ © ® °/₀ ª/c £ $ ¢

Family

A family is a series of founts related to the basic text roman face.

Normally a type family will consist of a minimum of three founts—Roman, Italic, Bold—and seven alphabets:

Roman caps, Roman small caps, Roman lower case
Italic caps, Italic lower case
Bold caps, Bold lower case

Many type families are considerably wider than these three basic fount designs, with versions in Condensed, Expanded, Light, Extra-light, Extra-bold etc. See the note on design variants below.

Series

A series is a complete range of sizes in the same typeface, i.e. Baskerville 8pt, Baskerville 9pt, Baskerville 10pt etc, is the Baskerville (roman) series.

Design variants

Typefaces can vary in weight and width. The relative weights of a type family traditionally progress as follows: Ultra-light, Extra-light, Light, Semi-light, MEDIUM, Semi-bold, Bold, Extra-bold, Ultra-bold.

'Medium', or 'nominal', represents the design in its normal weight from which the variants are derived.

The relative widths of a type family traditionally progress as follows; Ultra-condensed, Extra-condensed, Semi-condensed, MEDIUM, Semi-expanded, Expanded, Extra-expanded, Ultra-expanded.

'Medium', or 'nominal', represents the basic design.

Note that the more versatile third- and fourth-generation photosetters are capable of being programmed to create electronically almost infinite shades of variation to the basic design shape of a character, be it in slant, weight or width. Detailed knowledge of the particular system under consideration is necessary when specifying such variants.

Measurements

All printing measurements derive from the *point*, originally an imprecise unit of measurement used in the early days of printing for describing the body size of the founts of metal type in general use. Founts were described as 6-point type, 10-point type, etc, with each size having in addition its own name: 6-point was nonpareil, 10-point was long primer, etc, and the commonly used 12-point size was called pica.

Originally an approximate measurement, the 'pica' survived as 12pts when it was standardised at ·166044″ in the 1870s in America, and became the accepted—and exact—unit of measurement for all typographic purposes in America and Great Britain.

A European system—originally from France—had earlier taken a slightly different measurement for the point as its standard (didot point), and hence for its 12 point pica (cicero). The European measures are some 7% larger than the Anglo-American measures.

Both systems are in use.

The important measurements to remember for quick calculation purposes (Anglo-American) are:

Point size	Inches	Millimetres
1pt	·014″ (c. $\frac{1}{72}$″)	0·35mm
12pts (1 pica)	·166″ (c. $\frac{1}{6}$″)	4·2 mm

The exact conversion table is:

	Anglo-American		Didot	
Point size	Inches	Millimetres	Inches	Millimetres
1	·013837	·351	·0148	·376
3	·041511	1·054	·0444	1·128
6	·083022	2·109	·0888	2·256
7	·096859	2·460	·1036	2·631
8	·110696	2·812	·1184	3·007
9	·124533	3·163	·1332	3·383
10	·138370	3·515	·1480	3·759
11	·152207	3·866	·1628	4·135
12	·166044	4·218	·1776	4·511
14	·193718	4·920	·2072	5·263
18	·249066	6·326	·2664	6·767
24	·332088	8·435	·3552	9·022

Specifying style

I mention editorial aspects of house style in a later chapter. Here I need to make a few observations on composition style and the need to follow some basic rules. You should consider:

1. Indents: conventional practice calls for for new sections and the first line beneath headings to be set full out, with subsequent paragraphs indented, usually one em of set of the type being used.
2. Hyphenation: preference over breaks in specific words; lists of optional break points may be found in reference books such as Collins' *Gem Dictionary of Spelling and Word Division*; the number of successive word breaks allowed at line ends (two is normal); the avoidance of hyphens at the foot of columns and pages; the avoidance of second hyphens in compound words; the avoidance of hyphens in dates, times, lists of figures, names and sets of initials.

3. Letterspacing: whether increased letterspacing is allowed in order to justify problem lines (normally prohibited in bookwork and high-quality composition); whether automatic kerning is allowed, and if so, whether globally or just between character pairs determined by the typesetting system's program.

4. Vertical justification: whether interlinear space can be increased throughout the entire page to avoid a page make-up problem; this is not normally acceptable for quality composition.

5. Word spacing parameters: the ideal, minimum and maximum spaces allowed between words should be defined, or the typesetter's own default parameters accepted.

6. Page layout: define whether pages must be of equal depth across a spread, how great a variation from the standard page depth is permissible (normally plus or minus one line only in bookwork), and the minimum number of lines allowed in various critical positions (the last page of a chapter, before a heading at the top of a page, after a heading at the foot of a page). The treatment of line spaces which fall at the foot or head of a page should also be covered.

7. Widows, orphans and stumps: these must be defined, and the circumstances, if any, under which they are allowed should be clarified (widows are sometimes considered acceptable if the widow line is longer than half the measure).

8. Display or extract matter: the way in which this is to be distinguished from the text should be specified; conventional treatments include a choice of smaller point size, indents at the left or at both sides, or the use of space above and below the extracts.

The publisher must be satisfied that the typesetter understands the particular requirements of the house style before any keyboarding commences. A good idea is to dummy up a certain piece of text which includes examples of as many of the above points as possible, and have this set as a check by any prospective new supplier.

The time taken to establish a consistent house style can soon pay for itself; individually typescripts will no longer need a laborious and exhaustive mark-up but can be covered by the simple instruction to 'follow house style', leaving both copy editor and keyboarder free to concentrate on the particular requirements of individual jobs.

Design instructions

Part of a copy editor's task is to analyse each job in terms of structure, to enable the designer to represent accurately the hierarchy of parts, chapters and subdivisions in his typographic treatment of the material. Conventionally this is done by identifying the different levels of heading within the text with tags A, B, C, etc, which can be easily translated into the correct degree of typographic emphasis; sections of text to be treated as extract matter, quotations or verse are similarly marked for attention in the designer's specification.

At the same time the copy editor will mark for the designer's attention any special characters required in the text which might affect the choice of typesetter or typeface, and any peculiarities of the copy needing individual treatment; these might include tabular matter, simulated extracts from newspapers and letters, or any copy which will benefit from special layout.

Details of the number and type of illustrations are also supplied at this stage. If the job is to be made up straight to page the copy editor will need to mark cross-references in the text for illustrations, with an indication of how many lines of space are to be left at the relevant point to accommodate each one. This instruction will also have to cater for those instances where references fall too close to the foot of a page for the illustration to be included.

A common way of treating this is to tell the typesetter to 'leave xx lines of space as soon as possible after this point'. If the positioning of illustrations is too critical to allow this kind of specification, this is a clear indicator that the job should be set first to galley and made up into page following individual page layouts.

The designer will require some brief description of the work and its intended readership to ensure that the typography is sympathetic to content in choice of face, size and page layout; it should not be assumed that the designer or typographer will have either the time or the inclination to read every typescript that comes to him! A brief synopsis from the copy editor can save time as well as the danger of embarrassing misjudgements.

It is also helpful if a list of the proper names and foreign words used in the work can be compiled as a guide for the typesetter to the consistently correct spelling of such terms. Much of the above information can be usefully summarised in a form which is handed over from the copy editor with the typescript; the information can be helpful to both designer and keyboarder alike, and should help ensure both sympathetic typographic treatment of the copy and more accurate proofs.

Before the typescript is finally released from the copy editor a final quick check should be made to ensure that all instructions are clearly legible and that any potentially confusing comments or queries have been rubbed out or struck through. The typescript is then ready for casting off by the designer.

Typographic mark-up

The basics of typography cannot be learned solely from books, and skilled typographers rely heavily on a practical knowledge and acceptance of the conventions of design as evolved over the centuries. The temptation to break the basic rules in search of fresh effects should be resisted until these well-founded principles have been fully absorbed.

Main text

The choice of typeface will be governed by the designer's taste limited by the range of faces available from the typesetter chosen for the job. Rigid rules which provide typographic specification suitable for all purposes and tastes are not possible, but considerations of type design, appearing size and the suitability of different types for specific uses should be carefully evaluated.

The relationship of type size to measure will have a critical effect on the number of lines which either have to end with a hyphen or have very loose word spacing; a piece of advance specimen setting will normally indicate whether this is likely to create problems.

Subsidiary text

Extracts and tables can be set smaller than the main text, or with the left edge or both edges indented from the main measure to distinguish them from main text; half-line spaces above and below the extracted matter are also useful. These must be increased to full line spaces in those instances where the opening and closing of the extract do not appear on the same page, to avoid uneven alignment at the foot of facing pages.

Verse extracts can be handled in the same way or centred on the type measure if the verse form allows.

Footnotes are usually set at least two sizes smaller than the main text. They may be numbered by page, chapter or consecutively throughout the book, and may range at the foot of the page, with or without a rule to divide them from the text, or be collected at the ends of chapters or in a separate section in the endmatter.

Type area

The basic page style should be the first element to be decided in book or magazine design. The size and position of the type area relative to the printed page will be affected by the content, style and size of the book, and is usually specified as line measure in picas and points × lines of text in a certain point size and interlinear spacing.

Conventional margins for straightforward non-illustrated text work position the type area so that it sits comfortably on the page, with the two pages of a spread forming a coherent opening; in effect this means that the head margins must be smaller than the foot margins, and the back margins smaller than the fore-edge, or else the text will appear to fall outwards and downwards off the page. A useful ratio for the relative proportion of back/head/fore-edge/foot margins calculates these as 1/1½/2/2½ respectively. In practice it is normal to position type on the page by specifying head and back margins only, leaving the fore-edge and foot margins to fall automatically; it must be clear whether the head margin is specified including or excluding the running headline and folio.

Display matter

Chapter openings, part titles and title page require very careful treatment to achieve the right visual balance between type and white space on the page, and it is normal practice for the designer to create rough layouts both to help with the positioning of the various elements on the page and as a guide to the typesetter. It takes considerable skill and experience to produce freehand layouts which give an accurate visual representation of the required result, but fortunately there are several short cuts which can be used.

As a first step, draw up in ink a master grid of a double page spread in the correct trimmed page size and use photocopies of this for the different layouts required; nothing is more boring than painstakingly to redraw the outline details of the layout for every page, especially if you are not expert with a set-square and drafting pen! Similarly it is not strictly necessary for most layout purposes to spend hours tracing a more or less accurate likeness of type; more important than the exact details of the letterforms is that the weight and 'colour' of the type be correct, as these are the factors which will determine the degree to which the type looks comfortable on the page. The easiest way to achieve this is by photocopying an alphabet of the relevant type in the correct size from the typesetter's specimen book, and using typewriter opaquing fluid to convert this into the approximate shape of the words of the title or heading. Trim the photocopy of these 'words' as close to the image as possible, and move it around on the layout until the correct visual result is achieved; stick the type in position with spray adhesive, and re-photocopy the layout. The layout should then be cut down to the correct trimmed page size, as this is how it will appear in printed form, and the surrounding excess white paper can otherwise distort the finished appearance. The specifications and the positioning of the type are then marked on a copy of this layout. The positioning of chapter titling is often expressed in terms of a drop from the top of the type area, together with a note of the numbers of lines of text which appear on the page; type on title or part title pages is usually positioned by reference to the head or foot of the trimmed page.

The different subheadings within the text will be designed to reflect, in typeface, type size, style (bold, roman or italic) and position the hierarchy assigned to them in the copy editor's analysis.

A descending order of priority in each of these categories might be typographically represented by:

different typeface/bold of text face/italic of text face/caps or small caps of text face/medium upper and lower case of (same as) text face (rarely used since heads set in the text face look very weak) larger than text/same size as text centred on measure/ranged left on measure space above and below head/ space above head only with text on new line below/text run on in same line after head

All these variants can of course be mixed and interchanged in a way which may alter this rough hierarchy: a large size of italic, for example, will appear more weighty than bold in the same size as the text face.

It is conventional practice for at least the minor headings to be set in different weights of the face used for the text itself. Where a different face is used for headings maximum economies will be achieved if this is specified as a face which can be set in position from the keyboard of the text typesetting system; type from a display setting system will have to be stripped manually into the camera-ready copy or film.

In order for pages to align at the foot, the area occupied by headings and the space above and below them should always be an amount which is evenly divisible in terms of lines of the main text. Note that mathematically even space above and below a heading will cause it to appear closer to the text above than to the text below to which it properly belongs; a good visual effect is usually achieved by allocating space in the ratios of 2:1 or 3:1 above and below the heading respectively.

Running heads and folios

Running headlines repeat for reference the title of the book and chapter, usually in the following style:

fiction: verso – book title; recto – chapter or section title
(fiction is often however printed without any running heads)
non-fiction: verso – chapter or section title; recto – subsection title

Many variations on the typographic treatment of running headlines are possible; conventional styles call for them to be positioned either a half-line or full-line space above the top of the text, centred or ranged on the fore-edge of the measure, in text size italic or small capitals.

Folios may be positioned at the foot of the page, a half-line or full line space below the last line of text, centred or ranged on the fore-edge of the type area; text-sized figures of the text face is a normal choice.

If the folio and running head are set in one line at the top of the page, page make-up, if manual, will of course be cheaper than if they have to be positioned as separate items. Care is needed to ensure that the style of the figures and running head type harmonise: lining figures look better with capitals, while non-lining figures are more suitable with heads set in small caps or upper and lower case.

A well-designed book will always integrate prelims, main text and endmatter into a coherent whole by the use of related or harmoniously contrasting typefaces and a certain consistency of style. Whatever the layout of the book – centred or ranged left, symmetrical or asymmetrical – all elements of the typography should reflect the sense of purpose which lay behind the overall design of the work.

Composition order

Details of the above specification should be collected together in the form of an official composition order or specification sheet to accompany the typescript to the typesetter. This order will contain the basic typographic details of the job, with individual instructions marked in place on the copy and ringed to distinguish them from setting copy.

Layouts for at least the title page, a sample chapter opening page and a double spread of full text pages should also be supplied. Copies of all this material should be kept in the publisher's file for reference in case of query from the typesetter. If the first proofs seen are to be in page form, it is important that all instructions are precisely and clearly understood; ideally a specimen page will be set from a photocopy of the typescript while this is still being copy edited by the publisher and this will be used to provide a typesetting estimate as well as to check the design specification. If the schedule did not permit this, however, it is a good idea to request a specimen page at this stage, made up from the first batch of copy keyed by the typesetter. This can be approved or amended while the keying continues, and before make-up begins.

Proof-reading

The type of proofs supplied by a typesetter can vary widely and it is important to understand how these have been produced, and how corrections will be made, before proof-reading commences.

Depending on whether the typesetter is working with film or paper output, proofs will usually be supplied as diazo (ozalid) proofs or photocopies of bromide paper. Neither method gives a very good quality of image, and many apparent marks or scratches may be symptomatic of the proofing process rather than indicative of faults in the master image. Most photocopiers also distort the image by a small percentage, and although this may not be critical for straightforward text work, fitting galleys of type which have been 'stretched' in this way to an accurate layout is not easy: an enlargement of 2–3% will distort a galley of 40 lines of type in 10/13pt size by a depth of more than a line; which can cause confusion in the make-up of integrated text and illustration work.

Proofing by laser printer, which produces a dimensionally stable and accurate image is becoming increasingly popular but note that typesetters may choose to produce only a master proof by this method and subsequently photocopy this to provide bulk proofs.

Laser proofing devices can also be run in a pseudo mode in which they accurately reproduce the set widths of the characters in the specified typeface while not holding the fount information to allow them to reproduce the correct design of typeface. The result of this is that while the hyphenation and justification of lines on the laser proof represents exactly what will be output by the typesetting machine, the letterspacing looks very uneven and ragged; in effect the laser printer is outputting, say, Times but in Ehrhardt set widths. Both proof-readers and authors must be warned and reassured to avoid much unnecessary heartache and marking of proofs. Proofs should be marked with different colours of ink to denote the provenance of errors or changes.

Traditionally the following colour scheme has been used:

> Green indicates corrections to the keyboarding picked up by the typesetter's reader and marked on the proofs before they leave the typesetter. These will be marked on a single master proof and after photocopying they will appear in black on all except this master, so it is important that the marked proof is retained by the publisher's editor for the collation of all corrections.
>
> Red indicates errors introduced by the typesetter during keyboarding, and chargeable therefore to him.
>
> Blue or black is used for both author's and editor's amendments (AAs), which are chargeable by the typesetter to the publisher.

Any changes marked on a set of proofs by an author will usually be in one colour only, and it is the proofreader's task to distinguish between typesetter's errors and author's amendments, transferring these marks, correctly colour-coded, onto the master proof. It is helpful, however, if the author can be persuaded to use a blue, not black, pen so that these marks may be easily distinguished from the photocopied marks applied by the typesetter.

Ideally the proof corrections should be made using the marks specified by British Standard (BS5261: Part 2 1976); this is a comprehensive system which does not rely on the use of English words or letters and is particularly useful when dealing with proof correcting internationally. However the older proof correction marking system, BS1219: 1958 is still much the commoner system used within Britain. Both systems are reproduced in figure 3. The same symbols are used by the copy editor when marking up the original typescript before keyboarding.

Typesetters' readers often mark not only keyboarding errors but also queries against possible inconsistencies or errors of fact in the text. Reading departments often harbour specialists in the most arcane fields of knowledge and any queries raised are worth careful checking; even if incorrect, the question itself and a courteous answer on the proofs can only help create a sense of cooperative involvement between typesetter and editor.

Instruction	Textual Mark	Marginal Mark
Delete and close up	⌢/⌣ through character or ⊢⌢⌣⊣ through character e.g. charac̃ter chara̰c̰ter	⌢d̸l̸⌣
Substitute character or substitute part of one or more word(s)	/ through character or ⊢————⊣ through word(s)	New character or new word(s)
Wrong fount. Replace by character(s) of correct fount	Encircle character(s) to be changed	⊗
Changed damaged character(s)	Encircle character(s) to be changed	✕
Set in or change to italics	———— under character(s) to be set or changed	⊔⊐
Set in or change to capital letters	≡≡≡ under character(s) to be set or changed	≡
Set in or change to small capital letters	≡≡ under character(s) to be set or changed	=
Set in or change to capital letters for initial letters and small capital letters for the rest of the words	≡≡ under initial letters and ≡≡ under rest of word(s)	≡ =
Set in or change to bold type	∿∿∿ under character(s) to be set or changed	∿
Take over character(s), word(s) or line to next line, column or page	⎤	⎤
Take back character(s), word(s) or line to previous line, column or page	⎡	⎡

3a. Proof correction marks: extracted from the British Standard
(BS5261: Part 2 1976)

Instruction	Textual Mark	Marginal Mark
Raise matter	over matter to be raised / under matter to be raised	
Lower matter	over matter to be lowered / under matter to be lowered	
Correct horizontal alignment	Single line above and below misaligned matter e.g. / mi saligned	
Close up. Delete space between characters or words	linking characters	
Insert space between characters	between characters affected	
Insert space between words	between words affected	
Reduce space between characters	between characters affected	
Invert type	Encircle character to be inverted	
Substitute or insert full stop, decimal point, semi-colon or comma	/ through character or / where required	; ,
Start new paragraph		
Run on (no new paragraph)		

3a. (cont)

Instruction	Textual Mark	Marginal Mark
Centre	enclosing matter to be centred	
Indent		
Cancel indent		
Correction is concluded	None	
Leave unchanged	_ _ _ _ _ under character to remain	
Push down risen spacing material	Encircle blemish	
Insert in text the matter indicated in the margin		New matter followed by
Move matter specified distance to the right	enclosing matter to be moved to the right	
Delete	through character(s) or through word(s) to be deleted	
Change capital letters to lower case letters	Encircle character(s) to be changed	
Change italic to upright type	Encircle character(s) to be changed	
Reduce space between words	between words affected	
Make space appear equal between characters or words	between characters or words affected	

3a. (cont)

Instruction	Textual Mark	Marginal Mark
Correction is concluded	None	/
Insert in text the matter indicated in margin	⋀	New matter followed by /
Delete	Strike through characters to be deleted	ℐ
Delete and close up	Strike through characters to be deleted and use mark	ℐ
Leave as printed	· · · · · · · · · · · · under characters to remain	*stet*
Change to italic	———— under characters to be altered	*ital.*
Change to even small capitals	═══ under characters to be altered	*s.c.*
Change to capital letters	═══ under characters to be altered	*caps*
Use capital letters for initial letters and small capitals for rest of words	═══ under initial letters and ═══ under the rest of the words	*c. & s.c.*
Change to bold type	∿∿∿∿ under characters to be altered	*bold*
Change to lower case	Encircle characters to be altered	*l.c.*
Change to roman type	Encircle characters to be altered	*rom.*
Wrong fount. Replace by letter of correct fount	Encircle character to be altered	*w.f.*
Invert type	Encircle character to be altered	☿
Change damaged character(s)	Encircle character(s) to be altered	✕
Substitute or insert character(s) under which this mark is placed, in 'superior' position	/ through character or ⋀ where required	⊺ under character e.g. *x*⊺

3b. Proof correction marks: extracted from the British Standard (BS1219: 1958). Although this standard has been replaced it is still the most commonly used in Britain

Instruction	Textual Mark	Marginal Mark
Substitute or insert character(s) over which this mark is placed, in 'inferior' position	/ through character or ⅄ where required	^ over character e.g. x̂
Underline word or words	——— under words affected	underline
Use ligature (e.g. ffi) or dipthong (e.g. œ)	⁀‿ enclosing letters to be altered	⁀‿ enclosing ligature or dipthong required
Substitute separate letters for ligature or dipthong	/ through ligature or dipthong to be altered	write out separate letters followed by /
Close up — delete space between characters	⁀‿ linking characters	⁀‿
Insert space*	⅄	#
Insert space between lines or paragraphs*	> between lines to be spaced	#
Reduce space between lines*	(connecting lines to be closed up	less #
Make space appear equal between words	| between words	eq #
Reduce space between words*	| between words	less #
Add space between letters*	ǀǀǀǀ between tops of letters requiring space	letter#
Transpose	⊔⊓ between characters or words, numbered when necessary	trs.
Place in centre of line	Indicate position with ⌐ ¬	centre
Indent one em	⊐	□
Indent two ems	⊐	◫
Move matter to right	⊐ at left side of group to be moved	⊐

3b. (cont)

Instruction	Textual Mark		Marginal Mark
Move matter to left	⅃	at right side of group to be moved	⅃
Move matter to position indicated	[ ]	at limits of required position	*move*
Take over character(s) or line to next line, column or page	⊏		*take over*
Take back character(s) or line to previous line, column or page	⊐		*take back*
Raise lines*	⊼⊔	over lines to be moved under lines to be moved	*raise*
Lower lines*	⊓⊥	over lines to be moved under lines to be moved	*lower*
Correct the vertical alignment	‖		‖
Straighten lines	=	through lines to be straightened	=
Push down space	Encircle space affected		⊥
Begin a new paragraph	[	before first word of new paragraph	*n.p.*
No fresh paragraph here	⌇	between paragraphs	*run on*
Spell out the abbreviation or figure in full	Encircle words or figures to be altered		*spell out*
Insert omitted portion or copy. NOTE: The relevant section of the copy should be returned with the proof, the omitted portion being clearly indicated	⋏		*out see copy*
Substitute or insert comma, semicolon or full stop	∕ or ⋏	through character where required	*⸲∕ ⸴∕ ⊙*

* Amount of space and/or length of re-spaced line may be indicated

3b. (cont)

The Invention of movable Type

It is generally accepted that Johann Gansfleisch, who took his mother's name of Gutenberg to keep it alive, was the first European to use movable types. Records of lawsuits show that Gutenberg, with his partners, Johann Fust and his son-in-law, Peter Schoeffer, were developing the art of printing from movable types in Mainz, Germany, in 1450. It is also accepted that Gutenberg was developing the art as early as 1439. It is not known whether Gutenberg conceived the idea of movable types by himself, or whether he heard of the art as practised in China.

Although the famous 42-line bible has been largely heralded as the first book printed by Gutenberg, it was probably not his first work. The perfection of its printing was no doubt the result of perhaps many years of experience in making other works.

The first dated printing work from movable types appeared in 1454. This was an indulgence" granted by Pope Nicholas V to those who aided in the war with the Turks. The Pope's emissary went to Mainz to enlist the aid of the printing press to eliminate the necessity of writing each indulgence by hand. Evidence points to the fact that gutenberg was one printer of these indulgences

The Spread of Printing in europe

The art of printing spread soon to the other cities in Germany, and to other countries of Europe. Historians have listed the following printers who set up shop in certain cities on the dates noted

1460	Strasburg, Germany	Johann Mentelin	
1464	Strasburg, Germany	Heinrich Eggestein	
1465	Subiaco, Italy	Conrad Sweynheym	
1467	Rome, Italy	Ulrich Han	
		1468	Basel, Switzerland	Berthold Ruppel
		1469	Venice, Italy	Johann of Speyer
		1470	Venice, Italy	Nicholas Jenson
		1470	Paris, France	Michael Friburger

3c. A page of proofs corrected according to the British Standard set up in 1976

The Invention of movable Type

It is generally accepted that Johann Gansfleisch, who took his mother's name of Gutenberg to keep it alive, was the first European to use movable types. Records of lawsuits show that Gutenberg, with his partners, Johann Fust and his son-in-law, Peter Schoeffer, were developing the art of printing from movable types in Mainz, Germany, in 1450. It is also accepted that Gutenberg was developing the art as early as 1439. It is not known whether Gutenberg conceived the idea of movable types by himself, or whether he heard of the art as practised in China.

Although the famous 42-line bible has been largely heralded as the first book printed by Gutenberg, it was probably not his first work. The perfection of its printing was no doubt the result of perhaps many years of experience in making other works.

The first dated printing work from movable types appeared in 1454. This was an "indulgence" granted by Pope Nicholas V to those who aided in the war with the Turks. The Pope's emissary went to Mainz to enlist the aid of the printing press to eliminate the necessity of writing each indulgence by hand. Evidence points to the fact that gutenberg was one printer of these indulgences.

The Spread of Printing in europe

The art of printing spread soon to the other cities in Germany, and to other countries of Europe. Historians have listed the following printers who set up shop in certain cities on the dates noted.

1460	Strasburg, Germany	1468	Basel, Switzerland
1464	Strasburg, Germany	1469	Venice, Italy
1465	Subiaco, Italy	1470	Venice, Italy
1467	Rome, Italy	1470	Paris, France

Johann Mentelin
Heinrich Eggestein
Conrad Sweynheym
Ulrich Han

Berthold Ruppel
Johann of Speyer
Nicholas Jenson
Michael Friburger

3c. A page of proofs corrected according to the British Standard, 1958 version

Disagreements over correction charges are probably the commonest source of dispute between publishers and typesetters. To minimise these, the publisher should find out in advance how the typesetter proposes to both make and charge corrections, and if possible have these figures presented in a form which can be easily monitored. Depending on how corrections are made, more than one rate may be applicable, relating to amendments at the galley, page proof, or final CRC or film stage. The publisher should also keep a record of the changes made to a job by holding all returned proofs until the job has been fully invoiced; accurately colour-coded proofs are the evidence on which an analysis and settlement of fair invoice charges will depend.

On magazines and other work produced to frantic schedules it may prove difficult to keep a record of all the changes rushed through in the face of urgent deadlines, and although some of the more sophisticated typesetting systems provide 'housekeeping' software packages to compile statistics of time spent on the system for each particular job, such records can be difficult for a publisher to monitor on a regular basis. The only practicable solution is for both publisher and typesetter to operate in a responsible manner, with a degree of mutual trust in their professional relationship.

Some allowance for author's amendments should be included in all publishers' estimates. For bookwork this figure is often placed at between 10 and 15% of the total typesetting estimate, after which AAs can at the publisher's discretion be charged against the author's royalties; once a typesetter's invoice has been accepted as correct, the production controller will need to advise the editor of this correction percentage. Note that if very low rates have been agreed with the typesetter for the basic setting of a job, corrections may be proportionately expensive, and the correction percentage may need to be set at a higher level.

Illustrations

To ensure good quality reproduction, illustrations for inclusion in typeset pages should be chosen and prepared with care. If any doubts exist over the suitability of an original for reproduction, the typesetter or repro house who will be handling the origination should be consulted before camerawork begins; do not assume that all repro departments are capable of working to the same quality standards.

The following comments apply to monochrome illustrations which are to be combined with typeset matter, and which may often as a result be sent to the typesetter for reproduction.

Line illustrations

Where possible, try and insist on the following:

Artwork to be drawn in black Indian ink, with firm lines, on a smooth white board or paper.

Detail, stippling or cross-hatching not to be too fine, especially if a significant reduction from drawn size to appearing size is involved.

Artwork to be drawn no more than half-up (in other words, 150 reduces to 100). A slight reduction on camera helps neaten up any slight irregularities in the drawing of the artwork, but excessively large originals mean extra camera costs and the danger that fine lines may be lost in reduction.

Avoid the use of mechanical dry transfer tints to denote shading or tone; it is difficult to lay these tints evenly, and the camera will pick up irregular blotches in the tint which are invisible to the human eye. In addition, the tints are manufactured by printing onto backing sheets and, under a glass, it can be seen that the dots which make up the pattern are rarely uniformly and densely black; these may burn out to white when photographed.

Tone or tint work should be prepared using overlays registered to the base artwork by corner marks, which will be photographed separately and combined at negative stage.

Mark all sizing instructions on the face of the artwork in non-reproducible blue pencil.

Halftone illustrations

These will usually be photographic prints or airbrushed originals; often no choice will be possible as the original photograph will be the only one available, but if possible, specify the following:

Originals to be glossy, black and white bromide prints. Avoid originals with a sepia, matt or embossed finish.
Originals should be free from marks, tears or dog-eared corners.
Originals should have a wide tonal range, with even graduation of tones from highlights to shadow.
Focus should be sharp, and detail clearly resolved. Even so, applying a screen to a continuous tone original cannot improve definition; for this reason originals should be somewhere between same-size and half-up in relation to the final reproduction size to avoid blurring or loss of detail which may result from excessive enlargement or reduction.

Even where the quality of illustrations cannot be influenced, either because unique originals are involved or because the artwork has already been drawn, there is no excuse for compounding the problems through careless handling. Make sure that the following rules are rigorously applied by all staff in the publisher's office and by the typesetter or repro house:

Keep illustrations in protective envelopes whenever they are not being processed.
Keep records of which illustrations have been sent where, ideally through the use of self-carbonating delivery notes.
Never use paperclips or staples on originals as these will leave marks which, even though invisible to the human eye, may well be faithfully reproduced by the camera.
Write all instructions on sizing or reproduction onto a tracing-paper overlay and not on the back of the illustrations; always lift this overlay away from the original before writing. Use a soft pencil or felt-tip pen, never a ballpoint pen, even for writing on overlays: it is easy to forget to fold back the overlay, and a hard-pointed pen or pencil will damage the illustration.
Draw attention to any illustration which may require particular treatment, either due to a poor original or the need for a special effect.
Supply illustrations separately from the text, but keyed into position by markers in the typescript. Captions should be typed as a separate batch of copy, cross-referenced to the illustrations.

Illustration scaling

Explanations of the theory of picture scaling always make the process sound extremely complicated, especially to those not at ease with the mathematics of proportions. The best way to learn is to ask for a demonstration from someone with considerable experience of sizing illustrations as in practice the process soon becomes familiar.

The following steps cover the basic operation:

1. Determine the general shape of illustration required in the printed result (square, rectangle, etc). Decide which dimension (depth or width) of the printed result is fixed by the grid or layout of the page and will therefore regulate the area of the original which can be used; this might be a consequence of the type measure, column width or any other dimension from the page grid.

2. Compare the area of the illustration which should appear in this fixed dimension with the space the illustration must fill on the page and calculate the proportions of these two by dividing the illustration dimension into the page dimension. The resulting figure is the percentage enlargement or reduction factor.

3. Apply this factor to the second dimension of the original, choosing which particular area of the illustration is to appear. This area multiplied by the percentage factor gives the measurement of the area which will appear in the second dimension of the printed illustration on the page. If both dimensions of the area of the appearing image are fixed – as for example in a full-page illustration – the percentage factor derived from step two will regulate the area of the original which can be included in the second dimension as well: multiply the second dimension of the printed area by 100 ÷ percentage factor to arrive at the area of the original which can appear, and check on the original that this includes a suitable part of the illustration.

4. Mark all dimensions on a tracing-paper overlay, masking out unwanted areas of the original, and note the enlargement/reduction factor and the finished size of the printed result on the overlay, e.g. 'Reduce area marked to 80% to give 100mm × 64mm'.

5. Never allow the often frustrating mechanics of the illustration scaling process to overshadow the importance of producing a result which is visually attractive and relevant. Check that no important detail has been masked off by the scaling process and that no superfluous detail has been included. Refer to the caption or relevant text to verify this. Try and keep important parts of an illustration at a sensible size in the printed result, and avoid the juxtaposition of illustrations with wildly different proportions. (Figures 4 and 5 illustrate the basic routine.)

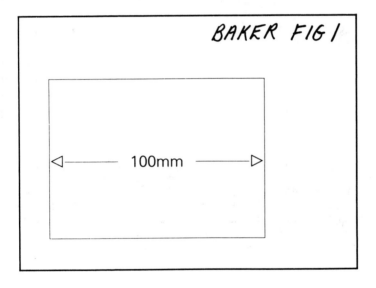

4. Picture scaling: a tracing-paper overlay on an illustration. The area to be reproduced is marked and sized, and the picture is identified with the author's name and the figure number

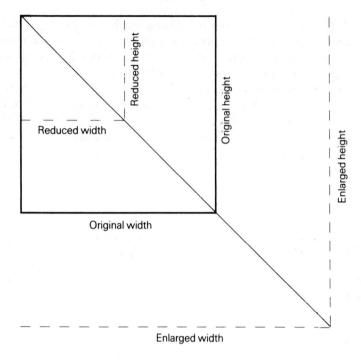

5. Picture scaling: to discover the height a reduced picture will be, draw a diagonal line from top left to bottom right corners. Draw a line from the left edge to the diagonal which measures the same as the reduced width. The vertical line from the top edge to the point where the width line meets the diagonal will measure the same as the depth of the picture when reduced. For enlargements, extend the diagonal downwards as far as you need to encompass the enlarged width

2

Style and consistency

The house style sheet is a list of instructions which can range between a single page of scrappy notes to a full scale book. But however it is presented, the style sheet in its basic form sets down for the use of copy editors those rules which they must follow in preparing copy for press, in instances where the normal rules of grammar or syntax or common usage permit more than one method of expression.

The style sheet may mention only a very few of such possible alternatives limiting itself to perhaps the name of the company's chairman and products or it may encompass a much wider range of topics, giving not only preferred usage in cases where alternatives exist but going on to give ground rules for good writing and clear exposition. The aim, of course, which may or may not be met, is that the reader's concentration on the final printed words is not distracted by inconsistencies or infelicitous expression in the text.

At its most basic, then, house style will consist of an index of local rules for, for example, the appearance of footnote references, the use of full stops after abbreviations, where capital letters should be used and so on, followed possibly by a dictionary of words, phrases and abbreviations which appear frequently in the books or periodical to which the style sheet refers.

The second stage, basic plus one as it were, is a style sheet which includes hints and instructions on writing style. Most of such instructions are don'ts rather than do's, and they might include such items as the avoidance of mixed or tired metaphors or the removal from the text of pompous or longwinded phrases where short, clear ones meaning the same thing will do just as well.

But some publishers go even further than this, requiring the words to be presented in a style of English which is recognisable as a trademark of the type of publication. An example might be the style of writing which distinguishes the popular national dailies in the UK.

The house style of *The Sun, The Star* and *The Mirror* is folksy and emotive. It reinforces stereotypes – all nurses are angels – all pensioners are indomitable – and so enlists the empathy of readers who find these portraits comfortable to comprehend and so continue to read the paper with which they can easily identify. This 'cutting your meat up for you' approach, which infuriates and alienates those who prefer the more sober approach of the 'quality' dailies is house style at its most extreme. And as an aside, it's quite interesting to look further afield at the very individual style adopted by some American newspapers and columnists, particularly *Time* which is renowned for its curious, and to many infuriating, use of inversion of the normal order of words in sentences.

But these extreme methods of presentation are encountered chiefly within popular newspapers and specialist magazines who fit their style to their determined readership.

Within book and the majority of magazine publishing, standard English prevails, and the house style sheet is devoted more simply to the elucidation of those areas in which alternatives exist and to the encouragement of clear concise writing.

What follows in this chapter assumes that your basic overall style is neither folksy nor pop.

Setting the style

House style, then, is intended to enable the reader to continue to concentrate on the content of the text without being distracted by inconsistencies, obscurity or awkwardness of expression. It sets out instructions on how to proceed in cases where there are equally acceptable options, and it may add to these the normal rules of 'good' writing.

Most book publishers and many magazines, particularly trade magazines, issue style sheets to their authors. The *Economist*, for example, has gone further and published a book on style. But this, while certainly the house style of the *Economist*, is really more a guide to good writing, containing as it does not only the *Economist*'s choice of alternatives but a great deal of straightforward guidance on concise and clear expression. And most authors are grateful for the help such a style sheet gives. You cannot force authors to follow it, but at least it serves as a warning that their manuscript may be subject to style changes if it does not conform.

What the style sheet is not and should never be is utterly inflexible. Any rule can and should be broken if its use makes the final text less than clear and accurate. Nor should it seek to blanket an author's own natural style. English is a rich and varied language and can be used in many ways. House style seeks only to clarify and enhance the content of the writing – not to mask or muzzle the author.

Few people are ever in the position of being able to set a new house style from scratch. More often, copy editors will find themselves working with an elderly and incomplete style sheet which fails to answer their questions. It may seem a mammoth task to undertake a complete revision, but it can be very satisfying from a number of points of view.

One is that once achieved the revised style sheet, if regularly reviewed, will save an enormous amount of time and irritation – and possibly costly proof correction – for everyone in years to come. Less noble but perhaps more persuasive a reason for taking on the task of producing a new style sheet is that it provides an opportunity for you to impose your prejudices on the printed word for months, years, or at least until another energetic copy editor revises it again to include his own arbitrary choices!

Most people whose job it is to process copy have prejudices of one sort or another. It may be dislike of particular words which from common misuse have now come to be accepted as having a new meaning. You may have strong views about the placing of semicolons; about Americanisms; about the proliferation of acronyms. Whatever it may be (and no doubt you are right) revising or setting the style is a unique chance to ensure that the words coming out of your particular factory are as clear, as readable and as well used as they should be, according to your own personal views.

Books

As each book is an individual entity, entire of itself, the first aim must be for consistency within each book. Indeed, for some publishing houses this may be the only aim, as every book is separately conceived and treated. Nevertheless, even then it is helpful for copy editors to have some ground rules. Authors are by no means consistent in their usages within a typescript, and the chances of costly omissions or mistakes in copy editing can be reduced if the editor knows, for example, that single inverted commas are always used for quoted speech, with double inverted commas for quotes within quotes. With such basics already decided for him, the creative copy editor can give his whole mind to the expression of the text, correcting its appearance on automatic pilot.

The next aim of a house style must be consistency within series, and here the same may well apply. If a series is, for example, a collection of books with the same basic topic – say detective novels – then each book stands by itself and may only need the basic ground rules. If, however, the series is more closely related and may be read as a series, then a need develops for a greater degree of consistency. The same abbreviations or acronyms may crop up in each volume, for example, and it will be confusing and irritating for the reader to discover COMECON in book 1 and Comecon in book 2, or worse still inches in the first and centimetres in the second.

Finally and perhaps ideally, the aim may be for consistency within the entire output of a publishing house. This does mean a very great deal of work for the style book compiler, as he must not only gather and collate his material but also seek and incorporate the views of his colleagues which will inevitably differ from his own. Nevertheless it can be done, and very satisfactorily too.

The other point to be borne in mind is the importance of retaining the author's individual style which must not be overlain by a correct but colourless standard approach. Unlike the newspaper examples quoted earlier, we are not seeking to retain a particular audience by our approach. Rather the topic and author dictate the style. Raunchy and racy stories need raunchy and racy expressions. In some novels, in biography and autobiography and in the more elegantly written professional texts, readers buy not only for the content but also for the sheer pleasure of balanced prose. That this is not lost, it is important that the compiler of the style sheet does not go too far in regulating the text. James Joyce versus the average style sheet would be an interesting contest. Knowing when to override the rules is as important as knowing when to stick to them.

Later in this chapter I have included a list of just a few of the basic areas which will need consideration in compiling any reasonably useful style sheet. Others you will think of for yourself according to the type of books you publish. I have also included in Chapter 3 a few first principles of what is currently accepted as 'good writing'. And this is of course the area where opinion begins to cloud the issue. Your view on what is a tired metaphor may not be the same as someone else's, and authors cling strongly to descriptive prose which to you may seem florid and overdone.

However, with caution and without dogmatism it is possible to spell out the principles by which we judge what we read and which lead us to want to read more of the same.

Once the style sheet is compiled, agreed and circulated to all the copy editors and other relevant personnel, you may want to consider preparing from it a booklet to be circulated to prospective authors. This is now common practice among publishers who are actively engaged in commissioning books. Topped and tailed by instructions as to how typescripts, illustrations and so on should be presented to the publisher, details of how an index should be prepared, proofs corrected and so on, and any other relevant information, this is very useful to the authors, and later to any freelance help you may engage (see Chapter 6).

Magazines

Unlike books, each of which is a separate entity and may be expected to appeal to its own individual audience, magazines expect continuity of readership issue by issue and are seeking to build some sort of two-way system of loyalty between the magazine and its readers. This is no less true of erudite professional journals than of the consumer variety. Without a core of regular readers, most magazines are dead.

Overtly, reader loyalty is built up in many ways which do not concern us now, but more subtly continuity of style underpins more assertive attention-holding devices. The regular reader feels comfortably at home with his chosen magazine because he understands it and is familiar with its methods of presenting the text.

Thus the first task of someone who is setting the style is to think about the overall approach; racy, homely, chatty, coolly professional: all these have their place among the many consumer, trade and technical magazines. Oddly enough, some of the most appropriate and thus attractive styles are to be found among the special interest magazines produced by amateurs for their clubs and groups. While often badly produced, misspelt and thoroughly scruffy, these sometimes contain writing gems simply because the writers set down straightforwardly what they want to say because they have no illusions or aspirations about fine writing. What they do write is clear and concise and in a style suitable to the readership: people with interests similar to their own.

Thus the first stage is to know and understand the readers and what they expect of their magazine. Its policy and aims can be simply incorporated in a statement which sets the tone for the text. Next we move to the compilation of a set of ground rules for copy editors which will ensure that there is consistency of expression within each magazine and within successive issues.

The rules will naturally vary according to the type of magazine, but they will all probably encompass such areas as the use and style of abbreviations, dates, the use of hyphens, inverted commas, measures, style of footnote references. Each magazine should then go on to list the preferred style for the vocabulary of particular importance in its own speciality: words and phrases which crop up again and again in the copy. Finally you may want to add some notes on basic writing for both news and feature material.

Adding and updating

The task of compiling the house style book is never finished. Only the most entrenched pedants maintain that standard accepted English does not and cannot change. As a pedant myself, I deplore some of the Americanisms and misuses of our language which have become part of everyday speech and writing, but I cannot deny that they have become widely accepted. Words do change their meanings over the years, new words are coined, acceptable phraseology alters.

The most obvious and most quoted example is of course the word 'gay'; but you might also consider, for example, the feminist influence which has made quite a number of respectable houses substitute chairperson (or worse, 'chair') for the no longer acceptable 'chairman' who happens to be a woman. And what about the universal use of 'chair' as a verb?

What all this means is that while a 'first edition' of the style sheet must be agreed and distributed, it should be the task of somebody – and preferably somebody who sees the task as important and not a tiresome chore – to begin at once to prepare the second edition, adding items omitted from the first, altering and updating.

Notes on additions can of course be circulated to everyone concerned. But eventually all the scraps of paper and scribbled annotations will have to be tidied up and reissued as a complete entity.

It really is important that this is done regularly. Staff do change and freelances come and go. They are more likely to follow a style sheet which looks as if it is considered important and which is put together neatly than if they are given a lot of bits of paper . . . or nothing at all. Indeed it is likely that anyone presented with a scruffy heap grandly entitled a style sheet will draw the conclusion, perhaps subconsciously, that you are not really too bothered about keeping to style so he need not bother either. The obverse of this is the new and conscientious copy editor, presented with a style sheet drawn up five years ago and never updated, who slavishly adds the imperial weights in brackets all through a recipe, when 'everybody' (including the author) knows that you decided last year to take the final metric step.

Here now is list of items you may wish to deliberate on before setting your house style. It is by no means complete, but may act as trigger for your own ideas.

Abbreviations

Obviously it's impossible to list all the possibilities, but here are some thoughts.

(a) *Organisations*

The names of organisations are commonly referred to by their initial letters. You need to decide whether you want to abbreviate them at all, and if so when. Will the abbreviations be in upper or lower case, and with or without full stops? It is fairly common practice to spell out the names of organisations in full the first time they appear in the text with the abbreviation to be used – often capital letters without full stops – in parentheses immediately afterwards.

There are a very few organisations which are known nationally by their abbreviations – BBC for example – and it is tempting not to bother to spell these out at all. But beware; if your book or magazine is to go overseas you cannot be certain that any abbreviation will be understood worldwide.

On the other hand, there may be abbreviations specific to the content of your book or magazine which will be recognised by all your readers. You may wish to specify these in your style sheet as exceptions to the spell-out rule.

(b) *Units of measurement*

Generally speaking, metric measurements are preferred but the most important point is that you choose one type of measurement and stick to it. Text which mixes both metric and Imperial measurement is unacceptable.

Then you will have to decide on the inclusion (or not) of full stops. It is perhaps sensible to list some examples: ml, kg, m, c, and so on.

(c) *Contracted words*

Decisions needed here include whether to contract words at all – Mr, Dr seem completely acceptable and the use of the full form would be archaic – but what about Prof?

Inverted commas

Decide whether you wish to use single quotes for speech, reserving double quotes for quotations within quotations or vice versa.

Capital letters

Generally, text reads more easily if it is not heavily larded with capital letters. You should decide when capitals are essential and use them only on those occasions. The titles of organisations normally take capital letters, and their abbreviations are usually capitals also (i.e. NATO, RCN), but the titles of people, except where followed by their name, can be lower case (i.e. the vice chancellor of Glasgow University but Vice Chancellor Smith). There are a few exceptions to this rule: the Queen (but any queen), God and Fellows all look peculiar without initial capitals. You must decide what is most acceptable to you and your readers.

Footnote references, bibliographies

Choose one style and stick to it. You can decide to number references in the text and list them numerically at the end of the article, chapter or book. You can put a name and date in the text and list the references alphabetically at the end. The only rule is consistency.

You should also specify how references are to be set out with respect to the order in which the information is to appear: author, initials, date, title of article, name of journal, or book, volume number, page number, publisher, etc. All references should include as much information as possible and it is worth drawing up instructions to ensure that missing information is obtained from authors *before* copy is sent for setting.

Dates

6 June 1987 or June 6, 1987 or June 6th 1987. Specify your choice.

Numerals

Specify when it is acceptable to use numerals and when numbers should be spelt out. A commonly used rule is that quantities which are followed by a unit of measurement (i.e. six metres) are conveyed as numeral plus abbreviated measure (i.e. 6m) except at the beginning of a sentence; while quantities followed by a common noun are spelt out (i.e. six eggs) until the quantity becomes too unwieldy (1721 eggs).

Full points

As with capital letters, too many points in abbreviations and so on spoil the look of the page and distract the reader. So consider whether the North Atlantic Treaty Organisation becomes N.A.T.O. or NATO and whether Doctor Jeremy Jones becomes Dr. J. Jones or Dr J Jones or a combination of the two.

Italics

When are you going to use them? Maybe for foreign words, but which? Some are used commonly in everyday speech and thus look odd italicised. The names of books, magazines, ships, are often italicised. List the occasions on which italics are to be used.

Hyphens

Hyphens have become unfashionable on the whole and the currently preferred method is to use one word or, if this is too ugly, two words. However there are still occasions when hyphens are essential to elucidation. Does 'three day old chicks' mean three chicks born yesterday or an uncertain number of chicks born three days ago?

-ise or -ize

Words ending in -ise or -isation can also be spelt with a 'z' in the place of 's'. Choose which you prefer and specify it. But 's' after y please, as in analyse.

These are really very few of the points which you may wish to include in your style sheet. When you have completed your list, it is worth adding a list of words specific to your subject where such a list can be made. This is particularly so with professional and trade magazines.

I have confined my suggestions to areas where each of several choices is acceptable; in other words, the very basic points which a house style might include. Later, in the chapter on copy editing, I have taken the suggestions list a little further with some notes on style and you may want to include similar notes yourself in your house style sheet.

The ten commandments of house style

DO	make it as complete as you can
DO	acknowledge that at least part of it is arbitrary
DO	circulate it widely in-house
DO	encourage authors to see and use it
DO	follow it
DON'T	follow it unthinkingly
DON'T	use it to obliterate the author's natural style
DON'T	consider its compilation as a chore but as a challenge
DON'T	forget to amend and update it
DON'T	allow design style to override text

3

Copy editing

Once at a dinner party I was attacked by a dogmatic scientist who, having discovered that I was a copy editor, insisted that my job (and I) were superfluous and that copy editing was a waste of time and an insult to authors.

But, sadly, the truth is that while many people have something worthwhile to write, very few are able to write it clearly, succinctly and unambiguously.

The job of the copy editor is to enable those who have an idea to put it across in such a way that as many people as possible will want to read it, will want to continue reading it once they have started, will understand what the author is trying to say, and will feel at the end that their effort was worthwhile.

What is the use of having a world shattering idea if the way you choose to communicate it to the world is so obscure, so ambiguous or so downright boring that no one can be bothered to read past the first paragraph?

English is a difficult language with a huge vocabulary and a complicated grammatical system. It is all too easy to confuse where you mean to elucidate.

By correcting spelling and grammatical errors, checking facts, clarifying ambiguity or infelicity of expression and introducing a consistent style, the copy editor clears away the distraction, enabling the reader to concentrate on what the author has to tell him.

Many, many articles and books would gather dust on the shelves were it not for the copy editor's skill.

There is another aspect: money.

The copy editor acts as the author's second thoughts. A well edited book or article should incur very few costs for corrections to typesetting. A poorly edited one will bear witness to the fact that the author who misspelt the name of the prime minister throughout his manuscript can recognise his error when he sees the name typeset, incurring for the publisher a corresponding bill for author's corrections in proof.

Finally, the copy editor should be on the look-out for statements which might be libellous. And if he is doubtful he will have the manuscript read by a lawyer. Some publishers' contracts now contain a clause making an author responsible for payment or part payment for such a professional opinion, but even if yours does not, the fee is likely to be a lot less than what you will have to pay out if you do publish a libellous book or article.

The copy editor in a book publishing house

Publishing houses differ in the areas of responsibility allocated to various members of staff, so not all of what follows is necessarily the job of the copy editor everywhere; nor does everything have to be done for every book. However, most books pass through most of the following stages before they are sent to be typeset.

We start at the point where a manuscript has been received and accepted for publication, the production department knows of its existence and has in hand the typesetting and printing arrangements. The design department has prepared or is preparing a type specification and a layout. Any major disagreements with the author regarding length, number of illustrations, and so on have been sorted out. Material which is copyright has been cleared with the copyright holder and wording of acknowledgements agreed. The manuscript is ready for copy editing.

The first thing to be done – without a pen in your hand – is to read the introduction, if there is one, and the first chapter.

Once you have done so you will know from the introduction the author's intention in writing the book and will able to use your creative editing talents to help him achieve his aim. From the first chapter you will discover how well the book has been written, whether the author has made an attempt to conform to your house style, the method he has chosen to refer to his bibliography, appendices and so forth, whether a glossary will be needed (for the book itself, though the author may have already included one, or for the typesetters if a large number of unfamiliar words occur).

In other words, your preliminary skim will tell you just how much work you will need to do to get the manuscript into shape. If it seems likely that a great deal of 'creative copy editing' is necessary – to the extent that the author will need to be involved and may object – it would be sensible to warn the sponsoring editor of the possibility in advance.

Now, at last, you can take up your pen (and it should be a pen, and not a pencil since some typesetters will not take account of pencilled corrections on a manuscript) and begin.

You will be reading, and correcting, the manuscript on three distinct levels:

1. Word by word, for consistency and conformity to style, correct spelling and syntax, inclusion of complete and correct references to bibliography and illustrations, accuracy of information as far as you are able.
2. Sentence by sentence and paragraph by paragraph for clarity and succinctness. If you have to read a sentence twice in order to understand it, then it needs to be changed. You should also be alert to the possibility of libel.
3. Section by section and chapter by chapter for sense. You are looking to ensure that the author's arguments are cogent, continuing and finally conclusive, that he does not introduce a new idea or character and then abandon it or him unresolved. In other words that the book hangs together as a complete work.

Good copy editing cannot be done in a rush. You need time to work your way steadily through a manuscript, checking backwards and forwards to ensure that you have enabled the author to say what he wants to say in the most readable and accurate way.

So beware of making assumptions. If the author's wording really is ambiguous, don't just opt for one meaning and hope for the best. Check with the author first. The worst sin in the copy editing rulebook is for the copy editor himself to introduce errors;

apart from being expensive in terms of proof correction, the reputation of your publishing house will not be enhanced if authors receive proofs containing errors introduced in editing. On the whole, authors are ultra-sensitive generally about the editing their manuscripts receive and they tend to regard your mistakes as proof of their feeling of being undervalued and unappreciated.

Moreover, it is not easy to enforce a contractual obligation on the author's part to pay for proof corrections over a certain limit (often 10% of setting costs), when even a small proportion of the correction costs have been incurred through the fault of the publisher.

Worse still is an error introduced by you and not spotted by the author until the book is in print. In theory, he should have noticed it at proof stage. In practice, he is going to be very annoyed indeed, and that can't be good for anyone. So when in doubt, find out.

Make sure that your alterations and instructions to the typesetter are legible and unambiguous; there's not much point in changing the author's words if your own improved version cannot be deciphered.

All the pages should be numbered sequentially starting from one. Any divergence from this system must be clearly indicated.

Diagrams which appear in the middle of a page of text should be photocopied, the original put aside with other illustrative material for the designer, and the photocopy reinserted in its correct place, with the diagram ringed and marked 'A/W' (artwork) so that the typesetter knows he can ignore it.

Tables can be typeset as they appear in the text, but they do need careful checking to ensure accuracy – do the columns add up? – and clarity. It must be absolutely obvious to the typesetter which column is which. If the table is very complicated or heavily edited you might consider having it retyped.

Headings

Chapter headings are obvious, but cross heads and subheads can cause problems. It is up to you to ensure that those which are marked up to be typeset in the same style – in capitals, or italics, or prefaced by A, B, C, or i, ii, iii, etc. – are in fact of the same importance. You cannot always rely on the author's typescript to indicate which are main subheadings and which sub sub-headings. In the same vein, using a lot of different styles to indicate subheadings of lesser and lesser weight may serve only to confuse the reader rather than help him.

Three sorts of subheading in descending order of importance should be enough for anyone.

If the book is to have running headings at the top of each page, then instructions for the typesetter are needed. Make sure the running heads are not too long to fit: a shortened version of the chapter title may be more appropriate.

Some authors open each chapter with a quotation. These should be checked for accuracy . . . we all tend to believe we know our quotations and many of us are wrong. I believe the source of the quotation should be given though not everyone does.

Tops and tails

Once you have dealt with the main manuscript, you can turn your attention to the prelims, end matter and illustrative material.

Preliminary pages may be supplied for the most part by the author, but they may be incomplete because, for example, page numbers will be added to a contents list at proof stage. You may, however, also have to compile some of the prelims yourself – or at least ensure that they are compiled – for the author will not include publishing details, ISBN number and so on.

Prelims must include some (possibly all) of the following:

Half title
A list of other books in the same series, or by the the same author or editor
Frontispiece
Title page
Publishing details – copyright note, date, publisher, typesetter, printer, cataloguing details, ISBN number
Dedication
Contents list
List of illustrations, etc.
List of contributors
Foreword, preface and introduction
Acknowledgements

It is usual to number these in roman numerals and you should indicate on the copy where a new page starts so that it is clear to the typesetter exactly what he is doing and whether he has all the material. If some is missing, to be supplied later, this should be indicated.

Most of the end matter will also be supplied by the author but you may feel a need to extend or amend it. It may include all or some of the following:

Acknowledgements
Bibliography
End notes
Further reading list
Material of a general informative nature not included in the text, such as tables or maps
Appendix(s)
Glossary
Index

The end matter may be numbered in arabic numbers continuing on from the end of the main text, or it may continue the roman numbers used in the prelims.

Whatever the end matter consists of, you should make sure that it is as complete as it can be (though the index, for example, will have to have its page numbers added at proof stage) and that any omissions are clearly indicated for the benefit of the typesetter.

Copy editing for magazines

As a copy editor on a magazine you are likely to be working to a tighter deadline than your colleagues in the book publishing world ... sometimes, indeed, with the typesetter's messenger or the fax operator breathing down your neck. On the other hand, you are more likely to have easy access to the journalist who has written the copy so that ambiguities or apparent mistakes can be clarified at once.

Much of the preceding section applies just as much to the magazine copy editor as the book copy editor, but there are a few differences.

Starting from the point where an accepted feature article or news report lands on the copy editor's desk, the first action must be to discover whether it is scheduled for a forthcoming issue and if so what space has been allocated to it. You thus have some idea of the urgency and know whether, when you take the next step of reading the manuscript through, you should be bearing in mind the necessity of cutting the article and by roughly how much.

You should also find out whether other articles on the same topic are to appear alongside yours, in case cross-referencing is needed.

Next you should read the manuscript to get the flavour of what the author is trying to say and to consider whether he has managed to say it, or whether some re-arrangement might improve it.

The manuscript should be read on three levels:

1. Word by word, for consistency of and conformity to house style, for accuracy of spelling and grammar and so on.
2. Sentence by sentence, for clarity and succinctness of expression and for libel (particularly important for those dealing with news stories).
3. As a whole, to ensure that the piece works as a readable entity.

You may have, moreover, a fourth level always in your mind and that is space. Apart from those, mostly learned, periodicals in which article succeeds article until an agreed total of pages is reached, it is normal practice to allocate each feature a particular amount of space. It is the job of the copy editor to ensure that the copy fits, by cutting or by indicating the need for extra material, be it illustrative or other.

While preparing the article, you may need to keep in the back of your mind that you will later need to write a standfirst or introduction for it, and perhaps suggest to the designer suitable ideas for illustrations.

Once the article is ready for typesetting, with all photographs and illustrations removed and labelled so that you know later to which article they belong, you should choose a catchline to identify the article and write it on the top of each page, together with the page number.

The catchline can be the author's name or a word which defines the subject of the article. I emphasise this apparently small point of procedure because it is in fact quite important. At a magazine typesetter there are likely to be a number of articles passing through at any one time and it may take much time and trouble to leaf through each one to replace a missed page. The catchline makes it clear immediately to which article a dropped page belongs. Moreover, when news reports are to be fitted immediately into a page layout, the catchline is written on the layout to show where each piece should go.

The foot of each page of the manuscript should bear the symbol 'm/f' or 'more' until the last page which should say 'end'.

Your instructions must be legible and unambiguous.

If it is the practice in your magazine for the copy editor to mark up the typefaces to be used, then you must do this too, following the design specification.

Headings

If the author has provided his article with a title, you should take the time to consider whether it might be improved. Very long titles can often be shortened with advantages both in readability and appearance, and what has been removed from the title can often be appropriately included in the standfirst.

On the other hand, beware of adding clever, 'snappy' or punning titles to serious subjects. What seems smart or amusing at that stage may serve in print to irritate rather than attract the reader and exacerbate the author's natural paranoia.

The author may have added his own subheadings appropriately and perhaps these can be simply marked up and left in the text. But it may be that they fall inconveniently when the page is designed, or that the designer wishes to add subheadings to improve the appearance of the page.

This may be a case when you need to remember the adage that design is the servant of content (Harold Evans).

The exclusion of the author's subheadings which indicate different sections of an article is usually a mistake. The inclusion of new ones may be wholly acceptable, but you must consider whether the suggested placing makes sense. And if you decide to add subheads, please choose words or phrases which match the tone of the article. I have seen very serious, scholarly articles broken up by such titillating words as 'sex' and 'disaster'. Those words may have appeared in the paragraph following the subheading but in a context quite other than that they convey by being used as subheadings.

Tops and tails

Once the main body of the article is edited, you will perhaps need to add a standfirst or introduction. This is intended to encourage the reader to go on to read the whole piece, and should be written in an inviting way. It's all too easy to write a boring précis of what follows. Try not to give the whole story in the standfirst... why should the reader then bother with the article? If you can tie the article to a topical event or controversy in the standfirst, then that's a good reason why the reader should read on. A standfirst in the form of a question is a useful device, but don't use it too often.

Also at the beginning of the article comes the byline or author's name. Double check the spelling and qualifications.

At the end of the article come the acknowledgements, the footnotes, bibliographic references and perhaps a short biography of the author. Make sure they are correct and complete.

Copyfitting

The most accurate way to discover how many lines or pages an article takes up is to do a character count and to use copyfitting tables or a calculating device.

But assuming you have neither of these, you can nevertheless make a fairly accurate calculation. First you must discover and write down for future use the average number of characters including spaces contained in a line of typesetting in the typeface and line width you are using. To do this, you will have to count up all the characters and spaces in ten lines of typesetting and then divide that total by ten.

Next you perform the same exercise with ten lines of edited manuscript, counting your alterations rather than the original version, and divide the total by ten. This gives you the average numbers of characters in a line of manuscript.

Next you add up the number of lines in the article. Multiply the average number of characters by the number of lines to give you the total number of characters in the manuscript and divide this by the number of characters in a line of typesetting. This will give you a guide to the number of lines your article will take up when it is typeset, accurate to within a few lines. If you are fitting, say, news copy into a page layout, then this is the preferred rough method. If you simply want an idea of the number of pages, then you need to find out, by counting, the average number of words on a full page of your magazine. Write it down for future use, then you can count up the number of words on one page of your manuscript, multiply it by the number of pages, and divide manuscript words into page words. Don't forget that you will need space for headline, pictures and tables.

Rougher still, one A4 page of double spaced typing contains about 250 words.

Illustrations

Illustration reproduction and handling was considered in Chapter 1, but here I should mention a few editorial points.

Illustrations provided by authors need careful scrutiny.

Do they match their captions? Do they really show what they purport to show? Do they really add anything to the text? If not, you may still want to use them to break the text up and to make the book or article more inviting. Are diagrams originals or photocopies? If the latter they need to be redrawn. Are they properly labelled, or will the labelling need adjustment by the design department, for reasons of style, inaccuracy or incompleteness. Will the labelling be legible when the illustration is reduced to fit the page?

There is no point in changing diagrams unnecessarily, of course, but if they need alteration anyway, it's worth considering whether part of the diagram would be better included in the caption or vice versa. For example, if the caption includes the meaning of various forms of shading in the diagram, then it might be better to include the key in the diagram itself, rather than attempt to describe hatching and cross hatching in words, or worse, include in the caption little drawings of cross hatchings.

Style

The first requirement of any material that is to be read is that it should be readable. And this is just as true of an obscure scientific treatise as of romantic fiction. The content may be more difficult to comprehend and the vocabulary specialised, but nevertheless the way the material is written must be clear, concise and as simple as possible.

Here are just some of the basic rules of simple writing, which you can use to improve the author's text:

1. Recast single long complicated sentences into two or more shorter ones. Otherwise the reader will have forgotten how the sentence began by the time he has reached the end and may become lost in a mass of subordinate clauses. Very long paragraphs have the same effect.

2. Replace pompous or polysyllabic words with their shorter equivalents. Events should start rather than commence; an unavoidable delay in despatch means he missed the post; the author may have participated, but so far as you are concerned, he took part. There are many more examples of words the use of which can make a manuscript seem less readable than it should be.

3. Make sure that the author's sentence construction is clear. Transpose his split infinitives and remove his hanging participles.

4. Prose larded with adjectives can be difficult to read. If a word seems to be fulfilling no useful purpose, cross it out. 'Very' is an example of a word used to strengthen descriptions which often has an opposite effect.

5. Do ensure that words are used precisely. 'Unique' is an absolute and cannot be qualified. A new innovation is tautologous and contemporary does not mean new.

6. Wherever possible verbs should be active rather than passive. 'It was decided by the committee' means the committee decided. The active voice is more vigorous and more attractive.

7. Metaphors often detract from rather than add to the clarity of text. But if your author must use them, do make sure he does so sparingly and without mixing them. An inadvertent mixed

metaphor renders comic even the most serious prose.
8. Replace jargon with a phrase in everyday use if you can
think of one. And while you are about it, delete 'buzz' words
and phrases, which date, and slang, which annoys. You should
end up with prose which is concise, precise, grammatical,
lucid . . . in a word, readable.

Relationships with suppliers

If your job brings you into contact with outside suppliers –
typesetters, repro houses, printers and the like – it is particularly
important that you remember that a less than professional
attitude from you may result in a unacceptable job from
them.

It is all too easy to blame outsiders for poor or late work when a
little forethought on your part would have made all the difference
to the success of the job.

Although most outside suppliers will acquiesce tacitly in your
belief that your job is the most important work they have, it is
rarely the case. They have other work on hand from other
publishers and all their jobs are carefully scheduled into a work
plan. If you miss your deadlines and fail to give them notice that
you are running late, it is quite unreasonable to expect them to
make up your lost time. They will try in many cases, but they
cannot put back other jobs to accommodate yours.

Outside suppliers need to know when work will arrive, when it
is needed back, and what it consists of. And if any of these change
between briefing and delivery, then you must let them know, as
far in advance as is possible.

Your instructions must be clear and unambiguous. If what you
get back is not what you were expecting, just take a look at your
instructions before you blame your suppliers. If they are anything
less than adequate, I suggest that a conciliatory approach
to asking for corrections, plus a private resolution to be more
professional next time, is more appropriate than grumbling or
shouting.

If your instructions were perfect and the job is inadequate, then
of course you are entitled to complain. Otherwise an attitude of
consideration and compromise will usually get more cooperation
and achieve more satisfactory results in the long term.

The copy editor's double check list

Once copy editing is complete, and you believe you have eliminated all errors, you should double-check that all the following have been done before the manuscript leaves your desk for the next stage. Omissions and errors now will result in expensive corrections later. Check:

1. Is the manuscript complete?
   a. Prelims – complete and marked where new pages begin, introduction, byline, and so on, added where appropriate
   b. Main copy
   c. References, bibliography, appendices etc
   d. Tables, illustrations, halftones, maps etc and their captions
2. Has all material not for typesetting (illustrations and so forth) been clearly identified and separated from the typescript?
3. Have all the folios been marked sequentially (and for magazines straplined)?
4. Do the references to tables or illustrations in the text agree with the numbers of the tables or illustrations themselves? And are all mentioned?
5. Are all bibliographical references complete, correct and consistent with whichever style you use? And do all bibliographical references in the text agree with the list at the end?
6. If there is a possibility of misunderstanding by the typesetter have you identified the correct usage in the margin (i.e. em or en rules, Greek letters, accents, number 1 or letter I)?
7. Has material included from other sources been acknowledged in the way set down by the copyright holder?
8. Have you identified and agreed any departure from recognised house style?
9. Have all spellings of proper nouns – i.e. people, places, and organisations – been checked for correctness and consistency?
10. Are quotations from poems, plays and other books correct?
11. Are words in languages other than English correctly spelt, including accents, and correctly used?
12. If there are to be additions at proof stage (references to

other pages, for example), then have you given instructions to leave a gap of an appropriate length?

13. Does the manuscript contain libellous material – or material which might be so considered?

14. Are all your instructions to the typesetter legible, unambiguous and complete?

4

Electronic manuscripts

It is the received wisdom – mainly among the not-so-wise – that the most cost-effective method of preparing material for publication is to persuade the author to 'capture keystrokes' on a computer or word processor and then to translate this electronic medium into typesetting.

The true situation is that, in ideal circumstances, an 'electronic manuscript' can save keyboarding costs and prevent the introduction of typesetter's literals; but in circumstances where technical or logistical procedures are faulty or difficult, the cost of translating one electronic medium into another can be higher than re-keying, and the administrative systems necessary to keep track of everything can involve the editor or production controller in considerable extra work.

As with many other aspects of copy prep, the key to success is to plan things carefully at an early stage so as to avoid muddles later.

A good starting point is to understand something of the technical problems which need resolving if the typesetter is to take the author's floppy discs and use them to output phototypesetting.

The first of these is the incompatibility between a word processor or micro computer on the one hand and a typesetting system on the other.

Incompatibility

With only one or two hardware exceptions (which for various reasons are not widely available), it is not possible to take a disc from a personal computer, put it into the input part of a type-setting system (the 'front end') and process the content into phototypesetting without further ado.

There are various reasons why this is so. Many are minor and create only relatively small inconsistencies in output which can usually be tolerated but there are four basic and universal 'standardisations' which need to be achieved through either hardware or software devices before one form of storage can be converted to another:

1. The character set (range of keys) available on the originating machine is likely to be smaller than on the typesetting front end and it will be impossible to generate some necessary characters and commands.
2. The program which controls the functions of the computer as it retrieves and stores text and performs other 'housekeeping' operations (the 'operating system') varies from machine to machine. Few typesetting devices use the same operating systems as micro computers.
3. The transmission code used to assign a numeric value to each character keyed so that it can be stored digitally may not be the same on one computer as on another.
4. The storage medium – the floppy disc, tape, cassette, etc – can have any one of a large variety of formats. Discs which have the same physical appearance may have other charac-teristics which render them totally uninterchangeable.

It is, unfortunately, necessary to understand something of each of these incompatibilities if they are to be dealt with successfully.

Keyboards

Apart from the old hot metal linecasting machines, it is safe to assume that the layout of the principal alphabetic keys on modern typesetting front end keyboards conforms to the usual qwerty arrangement, i.e. the top line runs 'qwertyuiop', the second line runs 'asdfghjkl', and the third line runs 'zxcvbnm'.

Above and beyond that, there is no guarantee that even two theoretically 'compatible' micros will have their other keys in the same positions and it is quite certain that a keyboard specifically designed for typesetting will have a unique layout. In addition to the likelihood that the typesetting keyboard will have a larger number of keys, it is also probable that it will have various special function keys which, when used in conjunction with the 'ordinary' keys, will produce special characters ... 'special sorts' in typesetting parlance.

It will have facilities for creating superior and inferior numbers, small caps, Greek alphabet and other esoteric requirements, but it will also need to be able to instruct the phototypesetting device to handle the mathematical functions associated with, for example, justification routines which require fixed spaces in some positions in a line of text.

Characters the typist thinks of as being perfectly standard are inadequate for typesetting purposes. The same key for opening and closing quotation marks is no use because many typefaces differentiate stylistically between opening and closing quotation marks. The universal hyphen as used on a typewriter keyboard is suitable for only one part of its normal function because in typesetting different lengths of dash have different uses as em dashes or en dashes, and the phototypesetter needs to see a different command string for each.

The RETURN key on a micro or word processor will instruct a lineprinter to advance by one line and move to the left hand margin. Hitting the RETURN key on a phototypesetting keyboard justifies the line to the right hand margin. To end a paragraph, the typesetter uses a QUAD LEFT key. And so on.

Operating systems

A computer's operating system is the suite of software routines which enables the user to load and run applications software (such as a word processing program), transfer data backwards and forwards to and from files and generally 'operate' programs.

As a copy editor you do not need to know much about operating systems except this:

1. Computers with different operating systems are not compatible.
2. Computers with the same operating systems are not necessarily compatible.

3. Computers running word processing programs with the same name may be using different operating systems and will then not be compatible (e.g. *WordStar*, a widely-used word processing program used in the writing of this book, can run on many different operating systems but the output will need different technical treatment in each case).

If we consider three of the most common micros used for word processing in the UK – the IBM PC and its clones, the Amstrad word processor and the Apple Macintosh – we will find that each uses an entirely different operating system so even the routines of retrieving files from memory are confusingly different. As we will see later, when we discuss various methods of handling electronic media, this is a problem for the editor if he fancies his chances of sitting in front of a bank of micros and simply plugging contributed discs into the right model.

Unless this is contemplated (and I advise against it!) simply note the three permutations of incompatibility listed above and be aware that they exist. Know that something generated under CP/M (a common operating system) cannot necessarily be retrieved or dealt with by another machine which also just happens to run under CP/M. Even the universal MS-DOS, the operating system of the IBM PC, runs on machines which, apart from anything else, often use entirely different sized discs for storing information.

Transmission codes

Each character or function which needs to be processed by a computer is assigned a unique numeric value determined initially by the designers of the microprocessor chip installed and its companion operating system. Consequently, internal machine code will vary from micro to micro.

Designed to achieve communications compatibility between computers, transmission codes usually conform to ASCII (American Standard Code for Information Interchange) or EBCDIC (Electronic Binary Coded Digital Interchange Code). The former is the most common code for microcomputers and we will therefore look at this in a little more detail; the latter is used on IBM mainframes.

Models employing a 7-bit data word (i.e. each character is assigned a unique seven-digit string of ones and zeros) will have as a minimum a code set of 128 items and it is safe to assume that the alphanumerics, punctuation and most of the remaining keys besides will be assigned identical ASCII codes no matter what the micro model. However, there can be occasional differences and some models have an extended 256-item character set in which the assignment of the additional characters may be purely arbitrary.

It is essential that the eventual recipient of any data knows the numeric value of each transmitted byte (or the character or function each will represent on arrival) and to this end the editor should persuade the originator to include a test file as the first item in any interchange. This should be constructed by working methodically through the keyboard striking each key in turn, storing this as a file on disc and writing out the results on a sheet of paper, e.g:

?	query
=	equals
@	commercial at
>	greater than

... and so on, terminating each example with the RETURN key.

On receipt this test file can be scrutinised and the typesetter charged with the business of conversion can compile a 'translation table' as required to suit his machines.

If additional codes have been added to assist in specifying typography and layout, these need separate consideration and I will discuss this later in the chapter.

Magnetic media

The size and format of the author's floppy disc (it is unusual these days for the medium to be anything other than a floppy) is usually the critical factor in determining the feasibility of using his output.

There are currently four sizes of floppy disk: 3″, 3½″, 5¼″ and 8″. Both sides of the disc are coated with a magnetisable material and

6. The four floppy disc sizes
Top row: 8″ and 3″. Bottom row: 3½″ and 5¼″

are contained within a protective envelope. 3″ and 3½″ discs have a plastic enclosure while the 5¼″ and 8″ versions use cardboard. The wrapper has cutouts for the drive spindle, read/write head and index hole (see figure 6). The two larger sizes have a write protect notch cut into the cardboard envelope and usually the disc will be *write protected* (i.e. it may be read from but not written to) when an adhesive tab is placed over the notch, though some device manufacturers require that the notch be uncovered to achieve protection. The two smaller plastic-encased discs achieve

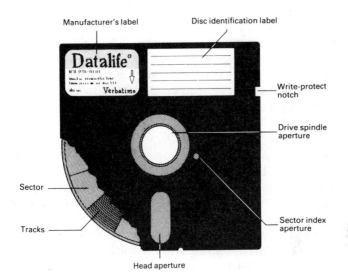

7. The structure of a floppy disc

and remove protection via sliding tabs built into the enclosure.

When the disc is placed in the drive and the door closed, the drive spindle engages with the drive aperture rotating the disc in a counter-clockwise direction. Usually the speed is constant though some discs revolve at varying speeds depending on which part of the disc is being accessed. The read/write head, moved under computer control via the operating system (see below), makes contact with the disc surface through the appropriate cutout.

The disc surface is divided into *tracks*, each track subdivided by a number of sectors (see figure 7), a 5¼″ disc (the size in widest use) having between 8 and 15 sectors.

Once the disc operating system has located the read/write head over the selected track (a simple matter of a measured lateral movement) it next has to locate the required sector. When the index hole passes the appropriate cutout in the disc envelope a circuit is completed via a beam of light and a photocell signalling the start of a sector. *Hard sectored* discs have a hole punched in the disc for each sector. *Soft sectored* discs have a single hole for synchronisation purposes, the start of each sector being determined by signals stored on the tracks.

Discs with different track capacities may be upward compatible, which is to say that single density discs can sometimes be read by double density models from the same manufacturer but double density discs can never be read on single density machines. Hard and soft sectored discs can never be interchanged.

Double sided discs can be used in single sided drives provided the user is aware that he must flip the disc over to access the second side, but care should be employed when using double sided drives ... while all discs are coated on both sides, single sided discs have inadequate quality on one side. Disc capacity can vary considerably. In simple terms one *kilobyte* (Kb) of stored word processing is equivalent to 1024 characters or about half a sheet of double spaced A4. The Apple IIe has a formatted capacity of 140 kilobytes per 5¼″ single sided 35 track disc while the Apple III, featuring a 3½″ drive, manages 143 Kb. The IBM PC also uses single sided drives but provides 360 Kb on its 80 track double density discs with options available achieving three times that figure.

A byte – usually eight binary digits (bits) – is the smallest addressable unit in terms of computer memory or storage. A disc capacity of 140 Kb is capable of containing up to 143, 360 characters, each in its own uniquely-labelled location. These location labels – or addresses – are maintained by the operating system as a sequential list, written in its own internal code, which is used to identify not only the start and end of each file, but also the exact location of each intervening element.

Let's take a file from a disc and copy it into memory for editing. What happens when the file, now altered in size and perhaps larger than the original, is written back to the disc? As much of the enlarged file as possible will re-occupy the original space and the operating system will then cast about, probably over several sectors and tracks, for space to contain the remainder, possibly left over from a previously edited (and now smaller) file, maintaining a register of the location address of each fragment. The final task is to write the address list to an index track under the file designation determined by the user.

When a file (or part of a file) is deleted by the user, only its reference in the disc index is removed. The original data remains intact until the locations it occupies are required for the storage of new matter. It may therefore be possible for the user to resurrect a deleted file provided that he has a suitable software utility to hand and that he acts before writing new data to the disc. In such cases, since the original reference to the file is lost, the software utility will relabel the missing file or files as FILE ONE, FILE TWO, etc., and it is to be hoped that, upon reading these, the operator is able to identify them.

To this end and to avoid possible confusion following a transfer of data to another device, each file should be clearly identified by including its title as the first line of text.

Unlike paper as a carrier of words, the floppy disc requires a deal more care in its handling. It is unhappy perched on a hot radiator, makes a bad base for ashtrays and coffee cups, hates close proximity to stray magnetic fields and is easily mislaid. The importance of extreme care in the handling and treatment of floppy discs cannot be stressed too soon or too often, for damage to a disc may not be apparent and may result in corruption of data everyone assumes to be accurate. The following points of good practice should therefore be observed without default and many will apply equally to the handling of tape cassettes and cartridges:

Avoid extremes of temperature (above 52°C/125°F or below 10°C/50°F).

Avoid magnetic fields. Keep discs away from TV receivers, hi-fi speaker cabinets, telephones, radios, calculators, etc., and exercise caution when carrying discs on Underground trains as the motor windings around the bogie axles are located in close proximity to the passenger compartments and create powerful magnetic fields. Carry discs or keep them on your lap. Better still, take a bus or taxi!

Never write on a disc label with a ballpoint pen or a pencil. Use felt-tip markers.

Never clip or staple notes to discs or to their protective sleeves.

Don't use discs that have had any substance spilled on them.

Always return a disc to its protective sleeve (and preferably also to its box) when not in use. Storing discs upright will prevent items being stood on them.

Never attempt to insert or remove a disc when the disc drive 'active' light is on.

Ensure discs are inserted the correct way up. Typically this will be with the label uppermost and towards you, but check with the system manual.

Take extreme care when inserting discs into drives. It is very easy to bend the disc by snagging the edge of the narrow opening.

Never handle the exposed surface of the disc.

Always make a copy at every stage that alterations or additions are made and ensure that software date stamping utilities, where available, are invoked and accurate.

Always ensure that a hard copy print-out is from the latest version and ensure that older versions, where retained, are suitably marked.

Keep back-up copies in a different location from the masters wherever possible. If possible, use a three-generation back-up routine: Set One, the latest creation, resides with the micro; Set Two, an exact copy, is stored safely elsewhere; Set Three, an earlier version, remains near the micro ready to become the new Set One, etc.

Don't crowd discs. Never fill a disc to more than 75%. Discs are cheap . . . replacement of missing data is not.

Establishing what you have

As may be deduced from the various problems outlined above, the important first step in handling any form of electronic output from an author is to establish what he is going to give you.

You need to know the make and model of the machine on which the text was keyed, the word processing program used and the operating system under which this ran. Additionally you need a test file of the character set, as described earlier, and preferably a short sample on a floppy disc together with a printout of this.

Then you can discuss with your typesetter or a specialist conversion house whether and how this can be translated into typesetting.

Establishing how you will work

The next step is to tell the author who does what and in which sequence. Let me suggest a few possibilities:

1. The author sends MS (printout) and floppy discs to the publisher, who edits the MS and sends this and the floppy discs to the typesetter, who translates the floppies into his typesetting system and handles the corrections himself, supplying proofs to the publisher.
2. The author sends MS and floppies to the publisher, who has a compatible micro, and who edits the MS on screen, sending 'clean' floppies to the typesetter.
3. The author sends MS only to the publisher, who edits the MS and returns this to the author, who corrects his files and supplies clean floppies and printout.

There are many other possible permutations.

I suggest the safest course on balance is to ask the author to work to option 3. This is not because I favour obtaining the last possible pound of flesh from the author but because (a) it is logical to send the typesetter the cleanest set of discs possible and (b) I don't believe it is sensible for an editor who is not a specialist in microcomputing to attempt to edit the wide variety of input he is likely to receive, even if the facilities are available.

We also have to consider the highly controversial question of whether editing on screen is sensible at all.

On-screen editing

I have deliberately avoided in this book including a section on how to edit material on screen. Firstly, there are so many systems available, with such varying characteristics, that it is impossible to generalise. Secondly, so much depends on the type of copy being edited and what degree of correction is involved.

Clearly, newspapers can be and are edited in this way but note that the characteristic of newspaper copy is that it is short. Magazine copy certainly can be edited on screen, but where this happens I have noticed that long features are frequently printed out first to be edited on paper before the screen file is amended.

Books have been edited on screen but it is the experience of several of the bigger book publishing companies that their editors find this difficult, partly because of the problems associated with the need to page back and forwards through a long document, and it is not a widely used technique in book publishing companies.

If screen editing is the method used in your publishing company then no doubt you will be trained to use it and will manage well enough to handle author's electronic input this way if the system can take it in. If not, I advise against trying single-handed to master all the technicalities involved.

Consistency the key

Whichever method of working you choose, the point to emphasise to the author is that consistency is all-important. I will discuss the use of special codes to help compensate for the deficiencies of a micro compared with a typesetting front end, but remember that whether such codes are employed or not, it is normally possible to handle a large amount of conversion automatically provided the copy is consistent.

It is possible in many cases, for example, to replace quotation marks created on micros with their proper typographical variants provided the spacing used on either side of the quotes is consistent.

In particular, persuade authors to use only one space after full points and other punctuation marks, to be consistent in the spacing between paragraphs, not to indent paragraphs, not to indent lists or quotations, etc.

The typesetter or converter can 'search and replace' strings of characters and spaces as long as they conform to the same style in each case but if they vary it is a long and tedious business seeking them out.

To code or not to code

One of the problems I mentioned earlier is the inability of micros to generate special characters or to issue special commands for typography and layout. This can be overcome in two ways: either the deficiencies can be marked on the printout (special characters may need to be written in by hand) and the typesetter can make them good or codes can be inserted in the original file. When in doubt, do not ask the author to insert any codes in his manuscript. Use conventional mark-up on the printout and leave it to the typesetter to convert this to typography and layout.

If, however, you can get hold of the author before he has keyed his first stroke; if you can agree with him a typographical style for the document; if you believe he will identify the structure and hierarchy of the elements of his work accurately; if you think he is reliable enough to insert codes correctly; and if you think there is a reasonable chance that you won't be re-writing the whole thing anyway ... then it may be worth thinking about a simple system for coding special characters and the main elements of typography and design.

There are basically three categories of character or function which need identifying by coding:

1. Typography: typeface and size, body size (leading), line length, justification, positioning, etc.
2. Standard characters: those a typesetter would expect to find on his keyboard, no matter what the system (opening and closing double and single quotes, em and en rules, fixed spaces in at least three widths, a full range of accents and fractions either supplied as complete characters or capable of being assembled from part symbols).
3. Other characters: the Greek alphabet in upper and lower-case and in roman, italic and bold faces, maths and chemical symbols, stars, 'bullets', boxes, etc. These would normally be called from a special file or 'pi' fount by entering the identification code of the required character or characters.

Micros are not able adequately to emulate many of the functions of group one and where equivalent or comparable features are provided by its word processing software such as underlining and emboldening (achieved by overstriking the required characters), these are crude and inadequate when compared with a phototypesetter's precision.

Some micros provide for opening and closing quotes but many do not and none have keys for em and en rules; they have only a few accented characters and even fewer fractions.

Many micros are now being provided with extended character sets bearing a mixed bag of extraneous characters ... a smattering of Greeks, an occasional maths symbol, even hearts, clubs, diamonds and spades ... and these might be used to represent their equivalent or other phototypesetter characters. Use of symbols in this way should be discouraged, however, as their interpretation or translation by a human agency could require frequent reference to an explanatory list.

The printing and publishing industry was clearly in need of a standard to cater for these device code anomalies, a set of commands which could be entered by the originator to inform the typesetter whenever a phototypesetter character or function for which he had no micro equivalent was to be inserted. Ideally, these commands would be legible on screen or in a hard-copy printout since a truly universal coding structure should be capable of recognition by human and machine alike.

What form, then, should such added commands take? Basically, any sequence of characters that will not be encountered naturally in the English language will work but for ease of recognition and to assist the learning process these sequences should be mnemonic in structure.

One such solution may be found in *ASPIC*, an acronym for Author's Symbolic Pre-Press Interfacing Codes. Conceived in 1983 by Tony Randall of Electronic Village Ltd., Richmond, ASPIC was adopted as a standard by the British Printing Industries Federation in 1984 and uses open and closed square brackets as string *delimiters* (i.e. characters which serve to mark the limits of the code sequence).

Available from the British Printing Industries Federation, 11 Bedford Row, London WC1R 4DX, *The ASPIC Handbook* details those codes that require explanation then goes on to summarise the entire code set in three main categories:

Essential ASPIC: a short list of codes adequate for many applications and consisting of codes for headings, paragraphs and change of typeface.
Standard ASPIC: taking the user further by adding among others small capitals, justification changes, dashes and quotes.

Supplementary ASPIC: providing codes for a comprehensive list of miscellaneous characters (asterisk, dagger, degree sign, etc.). This section includes three sub-categories:
Language ASPIC – accents and the Greek alphabet.
Mathematical ASPIC – maths operators, square root, etc.
Tabular ASPIC – defining, calling and terminating tabular columns.

In use then ASPIC could be employed to represent *all* phototypesetter functions and characters as far as these are known and understood by the encoder. Even where a micro equivalent is present – a fraction perhaps or an accented character – the ASPIC variant should be used to maintain consistency.

Figure 8 shows ASPIC in use ... its inclusion in a word processed file (figure 8a) and the result after translation and output from a phototypesetter (figure 8b). In this instance output is in 8 point Times Medium on a 10 point body and set to a justified length of 22 ems, but the same original ASPIC could just as readily have been made to generate completely different typography. The originator/encoder will probably be unaware, in any event, of the typesetting specification at the keying stage.

From the examples given in figure 8a it will be seen that ASPIC is for the greater part mnemonic and the average typist should have little trouble in committing the essential and standard elements to memory in a matter of days.

There are many other coding systems in existence and some are just as effective. If your favourite typesetter has a preference you may as well adopt it! But here's a sample of ASPIC as an indication:

Essential ASPIC

Headings		**Founts**
[h1]	Starts first level heading	[r] Roman
[1x]	Ends first level heading	[i] Italic
[h2]	Starts second level heading	[b] Bold
[2x]	Ends second level heading	

```
[ h1]"CLASSIC'  CARS[ 1c][ 1x][ h2] The
Ford  Zodiac[ 1c][ 2x][ t1][ b] Born  in
the  late  '50s,  the  Ford
[ bi] Zodiac[ b]  and  its  lower-
specification  sisters  the
[ bi] Zephyr[ b]  and  [ bi] Consul[ b],
are  not  long  enough  in  the  tooth  to
have  achieved  true  veteran
status[ ][ r] Nonetheless,  these
elderly  ladies  are  often  to  be
found  displayed  by  their  proud
owners  at  rallies  and  county  shows
up  and  down  the  country. ]]
[ h3] Reliable[ 1c][ 3x][ t1] Powered  by
the  very  reliable  if  somewhat
unspectacular  Ford  105E  engine  [ md]
a  "classic'  in  its  own  right  [ md]
the  [ i] Zodiac[ r]'s  2.2  litres
proved  adequate  to  haul  the
vehicle's  1[ p123]  ton  kerbside
weight  without  undue  effort.[ ]
```

8a. A word processed file incorporating ASPIC codes

'CLASSIC' CARS
The Ford Zodiac

Born in the late '50s, the Ford *Zodiac* and its lower-specification sisters the *Zephyr* and *Consul*, are not long enough in the tooth to have achieved true veteran status.

Nonetheless, these elderly ladies are often to be found displayed by their proud owners at rallies and county shows up and down the country.

Reliable

Powered by the very reliable if somewhat unspectacular Ford 105E engine — a 'classic' in its own right — the *Zodiac*'s 202 litres proved adequate to haul the vehicle's 1½ ton kerbside weight without undue effort.

8b. The typeset version after translation of the interfacing codes

Text		Paragraph endings	
[t1]	Starts first level text	]]	New para, without indent
[t2]	Starts second level text	[]	New para, with indent

SGML

An alternative to coding (or marking up) manuscripts for typography is to use Standard Generalised Mark-up Language (SGML).

In SGML, for which a Draft International Standard was produced recently, the logical structure of a file of text is identified.

Coding systems such as ASPIC are designed to encode data specifically for a single purpose. Thus:

[b]Seaview Hotel[lc]
[i]Margate, Kent[lc]
[r]AA approved[lc]
[bi]36 rooms (12 with bath)[lc]
[i]From £16.50 per night[lc]

might be output as:

Seaview Hotel
Margate, Kent
AA approved
36 rooms (12 with bath)
From £16.50 per night

As these are essentially typesetting codes they might just as easily result in:

Seaview Hotel
Margate, Kent
AA approved
36 rooms (12 with bath)
From £16.50 per night

or, indeed, any other typeface family specified by the designer but they are of little use for identifying structure because, for example, the town and the room rate have the same coding.

SGML is a generic coding system designed to identify structure rather than specifying typography. Thus our example might be encoded as:

<hotel>Seaview Hotel
<town>Margate
<county>Kent
<classification>AA approved
<accommodation>36 rooms
<additional features>12 with bath
<rates>From £16.50 <period>per night

These labels might be used not only to apply typography (which can be varied according to the typesetting interpretation of the elements of the structure) but also to place each element accurately within a database which could then also output the file in a different medium ... say as an on-line database where searches could be conducted for rooms with cheap rates.

The SGML standard does not use the codes in my example, of course, but has a comprehensive set of codes to identify the logical structure of a wide range of documents, including all the elements which would normally be found in books, journals, etc.

This is arguably the truly logical way to mark up or code any document, given that its structure must be the true starting point for any display purposes. The technique needs a book to itself; meanwhile, much valuable work has been done by the Print Industries Research Association and information and training are available from PIRA.

Translation and communication

It is very unlikely that the editor uninitiated in the mysteries of 'comms' will want to attempt the conversion process from one machine to another himself, and I do not propose to go into this in detail, but it may be helpful to understand something of the various methods which can be employed.

If, as is likely, the author's discs cannot be slotted into the typesetting front end in their raw state, there are several methods of transferring the data onto the appropriate medium (i.e. from the word processor discs to the storage medium of the typesetting device). Some of the common techniques are considered below.

Multi disc conversion

Much progress has been made in the last couple of years in developing machines which can read data from one format of disc, translate it as necessary, and transfer it to a different format. Such machines look like microprocessors with a variety of disc drives and they run programs which present the user with menus of choices of the 'From ... to ... ' type.

These are quite complicated and expensive machines, normally used by typesetters or specialist conversion houses, but in the hands of experts can achieve good results provided reliable information is given about the source material and the target medium.

If this route is followed, the publisher simply gives the discs, printout and a sheet of information to the conversion house, which in due course supplies discs suitable for the typesetting system.

Telecommunications

Using a modem, communications software and a telephone line, it is possible to send a file from a microprocessor down the phone line and into the receiving device. Suitable equipment and expertise naturally have to be available to achieve this and it is best left to the experts.

Data transporting

Known in the trade as 'milking machines', data transporters are really glorified cassette recorders (although some use discs) which 'record' the data from the originating micro through a cable connection, physically transport it to the typesetting system, and 'play it back' at that end.

The most difficult part of the operation is normally connecting cables correctly at each end and discovering how to persuade the machines to send and receive it. As a technique it is relatively simple, but of course it does involve physical transportation of the machine to each site.

The translation of any codes which exist in the original files or the 'search and replace' routines which are used to replace type-writing conventions with typesetting commands can be handled either during transmission of data by running programs which perform these functions, or as a separate operation using special software on the typesetting system.

The need to administrate

As pointed out at the opening of this chapter, converting one form of medium to another can save time and money or cost it. Much depends on the material being processed but more is governed by the administrative efficiency with which it is handled.

At the risk of being tedious it is sensible to repeat the point that good information about the files being worked on is essential. As a minimum, the publisher should be able to give his supplier of conversion services:

The make and model of the originating machine
The operating system in use
The word processing program
A test file of the character set
A printout of the files
A list of the discs and what they contain
A list of the spacing conventions used for punctuation, paragraphs, etc.

5

CRC and DTP

With the advent of electronic typewriters and word processors it has become acceptable practice with some forms of publishing to use the author's typed manuscript as camera-ready artwork and reduce it to fit a book or journal sized page.

Whether this is aesthetically acceptable is a decision to be made by the publisher and his sales department. Whether it is a practical method of operation depends partly on the likely level of correction to the original manuscript, and partly on the facilities for and keenness about re-typing the defaced artwork after editing.

If there is an assumption that the author will prepare pristine material in an exemplary condition for publication, then there is no problem. I leave it to the reader to form an opinion on whether or not this is likely. If a more pragmatic view is taken of the likely level of correction, then someone must be prepared to re-type the manuscript and this may or may not be cheaper than conventional typesetting depending on the financial arrangements for paying for this work.

Whatever the assumptions, it must be agreed between author and publisher at the outset what processes of editing and correction will take place and who will perform them.

If it is accepted that the original manuscript is simply a draft and that there will be a completely re-typed final version, then it matters not how the original is presented, within the normal standards of presenting copy for editing. The final typed version, however, will need to conform to style in a number of important respects.

Conformity to style

House style will need to be agreed in detail. A proper style book should be prepared and must be followed by the author and editor scrupulously. It may be possible to make corrections fairly simply on a word processor but it will be very irritating to re-type a complete page on an electric typewriter because an abbreviation has been handled incorrectly.

As with keying electronic manuscripts, there will need to be consistent rules for spacing around punctuation and these may not be what the typist learnt at secretarial college. Additionally the presentational style for headings, footnotes, lists, tables, emphasised text of one sort or another, and so on, will need agreeing, specifying and possibly modifying to suit the facilities which exist on the author's own machine.

You will need to specify what must happen when characters are needed which cannot be generated on the typewriter – hand-drawn, Letraset, etc – and do not forget in this respect the problematic use of hyphens and dashes . . . not the same character on the printed page.

You will need to agree whether any parts of the manuscript are to be re-set typographically. This may be decided for chapter headings, etc. If so, instruct the typist on the correct space to leave.

Preparation

The first decision to be made is the original typed area and the degree of reduction necessary to achieve the correct text area on the final printed page.

Remember there are at least three different typewriter type sizes in current use – 10 pitch, 12 pitch and 15 pitch – and these calculations will vary according to the size employed on a particular manuscript. With word processed material it is also useful to see a sample of the particular typeface proposed since the 'appearing size' of some word processor faces can vary dramatically.

My experience is that there is no substitute for trial and error in working out original and reduced sizes. Have a set of originals typed with different text areas and margins, ask a repro supplier to reduce them to the printed page text area and then form a view on what works best.

When a word processor or electronic typewriter is being used it will be necessary to decide whether you want the text justified or unjustified. Remember that, with the exception of some desktop publishing systems mentioned below, the spacing used to achieve justification on most word processors and electronic typewriters is rather crude and may result in text which is really quite difficult to read.

As an example, figures 9 and 10 overleaf show two pages of word processed copy produced with conventional margins on A4-sized paper and reduced to the text area of this book. Figure 9 has been justified and figure 10 has ragged right margins.

Ensure good quality, white paper is used for output and, if possible, a carbon ribbon is used rather than a fabric ribbon which varies in intensity of image.

Desktop publishing

Desktop publishing is really a generic marketing term used to describe hardware and software which can replicate typefaces and sizes in their true characteristics on screen and then output the result to a laser printer which can reproduce the copy in a low resolution version of the true typography.

WYSIWYG (What You See Is What You Get) is the term used to describe the relatively new facility of seeing an accurate representation of the finished result on screen.

There are two ways to use desktop publishing systems:

1. The output from the laser printer can be used as camera-ready artwork.
2. If the DTP system and the laser printer have the appropriate software, the laser printer can be used as a proofing device to show exactly what result will be obtained when the files are processed through an industry-standard typesetting device.

DTP as CRC

The current generation of laser printers (as distinct from laser phototypesetters) output at a resolution of 300 dots to the linear

CRC and DTP

With the advent of electronic typewriters and word processors it has become acceptable practice with some forms of publishing to use the author's typed manuscript as camera-ready artwork and reduce it to fit a book or journal sized page.

Whether this is aesthetically acceptable is a decision to be made by the publisher and his sales department. Whether it is a practical method of operation depends partly on the likely level of correction to the original manuscript, partly on the facilities for and keenness about re-typing the defaced artwork after editing.

If there is an assumption that the author will prepare pristine material in an examplary condition for publication, then there is no problem. I leave it to the reader to form an opinion on whether or not this is likely. If a more pragmatic view is taken of the likely level of correction, then someone must be prepared to re-type the manuscripts and this may or may not be cheaper than conventional typesetting depending on the financial arrangements for paying for this work.

Whatever the assumptions, it must be agreed between author and publisher at the outset what processes of editing and correction will take place and who will perform them.

If it is accepted that the original manuscript is simply a draft and that there will be a completely re-typed final version, then it matters not how the original is presented, within the normal standards of presenting copy for editing. The final typed version, however, will need to conform to style in a number of important respects.

CONFORMITY TO STYLE

House style will need to be agreed in detail. A proper style book should be prepared and must be followed by the author and editor scrupulously. It may be possible to make corrections fairly simply on a word processor but it will be very irritating to re-type a complete page on an electric typewriter because an abbreviation has been handled incorrectly.

As with keying electronic manuscripts, there will need to be consistent rules for spacing around punctuation and these may not be what the typist learnt at secretarial college. Additionally the presentational style for headings, footnotes, lists, tables, emphasised text of one sort or another, and so on, will need agreeing, specifying and possibly modifying to suit the facilities which exist on the author's own machine.

9. Word processed text with a justified right margin

CRC and DTP

With the advent of electronic typewriters and word
processors it has become acceptable practice with some
forms of publishing to use the author's typed manuscript
as camera-ready artwork and reduce it to fit a book or
journal sized page.

Whether this is aesthetically acceptable is a decision to
be made by the publisher and his sales department.
Whether it is a practical method of operation depends
partly on the likely level of correction to the original
manuscript, partly on the facilities for and keenness
about re-typing the defaced artwork after editing.

If there is an assumption that the author will prepare
pristine material in an examplary condition for
publication, then there is no problem.   I leave it to
the reader to form an opinion on whether or not this is
likely.   If a more pragmatic view is taken of the likely
level of correction, then someone must be prepared to re-
type the manuscripts and this may or may not be cheaper
than conventional typesetting depending on the financial
arrangements for paying for this work.

Whatever the assumptions, it must be agreed between
author and publisher at the outset what processes of
editing and correction will take place and who will
perform them.

If it is accepted that the original manuscript is simply
a draft and that there will be a completely re-typed
final version, then it matters not how the original is
presented, within the normal standards of presenting copy
for editing.   The final typed version, however, will need
to conform to style in a number of important respects.

CONFORMITY TO STYLE

House style will need to be agreed in detail.   A proper
style book should be prepared and must be followed by the
author and editor scrupulously.   It may be possible to
make corrections fairly simply on a word processor but it
will be very irritating to re-type a complete page on an
electric typewriter because an abbreviation has been
handled incorrectly.

10. Word processed text with right margin unjustified

inch. This compares with the lowest normal resolution of a phototypesetting machine at around 1000 dots or equivalent (however this is an area where improvements are being made constantly and printers with resolutions of 400 or even 800 dots per inch may soon be with us).

At present the laser printer output is inferior in terms of the quality of resolution of the finished result. For some purposes it will be adequate, for some purposes it won't be. The only reliable method of determination is to ask the author (or, more likely, university department or corporate organisation) which has such a system to send you sample sheets to examine.

To give you some guidelines, figures 11 and 12 show output from, on the one hand, a laser printer and, on the other, a typical phototypesetting machine. The 'fuzzy edges' of the type are clearly visible on the larger sizes, not so apparent on the smaller.

If laser printer output is acceptable in terms of clarity of image, examine an example of the justified output. Some of the earlier DTP software had inadequate H&J routines which create inter-word spacing which may not be acceptable in all circumstances.

If this criterion is also met, then proceed as if the author were your typesetter... because that is, effectively, the role he is playing. Go through the normal proofing and correcting routines until you have the finished result you require.

DTP as a typesetting front end

If a DTP system uses a 'page description language', such as Post-Script, which is compatible with an industry-standard typesetting system (and this is possible with several widely-used phototype-setters, including some of the Monotype and Linotype models), then the output from the laser printer will be a proof in correct typographical form but at a low resolution of what will be achieved if the files are subsequently processed through the phototypesetting system.

In this case, the author is really still performing most of the traditional functions of a typesetter but, if you elect to use the higher quality of a typesetter output device, you will need to arrange with a typesetting company to output the final pages once the author has produced a set of correct proofs from his corrected and updated files.

60pt 36pt 24pt

18pt 14pt 12pt 10pt 8pt 6pt 4.5pt

Times Roman *Times Italic*

Times Bold *Times Bold Italic*

Rockwell Light **Rockwell Bold**

Optima Medium *Goudy Heavyface Italic*

Plantin *Plantin Italic* Plantin Bold

Bembo *Bembo Italic* **Bembo Bold**

Baskerville *Baskerville Italic* **Baskerville Bold**

Century Schoolbook *Century Schoolbook Italic*

Eras Ultra Bold **Franklin Gothic Demi**

☆ ☆ ★ ★ ★ □ □ □ ■ ■

☞ ☏ ✂ · · · · · ✂ ☎ ✈

α β γ δ ε ζ η θ ϑ

11. Output from a laser printer

60pt 36pt 24pt

18pt 14pt 12pt 10pt 8pt 6pt 4.5pt

Times Roman   *Times Italic*

Times Bold   ***Times Bold Italic***

Rockwell Light   **Rockwell Bold**

Optima Medium   ***Goudy Heavyface Italic***

Plantin   *Plantin Italic*   **Plantin Bold**

Bembo   *Bembo Italic*   **Bembo Bold**

Baskerville   *Baskerville Italic*   **Baskerville Bold**

Century Schoolbook   *Century Schoolbook Italic*

Eras Ultra Bold   **Franklin Gothic Demi**

☆ ☆ ★ ★ ★   □ □ □ ■ ■

☞ ☏ ✂--------➤ ☎ ☜

α β γ δ ε ζ η θ ϑ

12. Output from a phototypesetter

If you choose to follow this route, discuss the matter with your typesetter before you embark on the journey. The manufacturer of the DTP system will claim compatibility with one or more output devices, but beware: there are various parameters on typesetting output machines which can be unique to that particular machine as it has been set up by the typesetter. This need not necessarily cause serious problems but it is necessary to check with your typesetter and probably to run through a short test file.

DTP systems are evolving rapidly. New, relatively sophisticated software for the IBM PC and its compatibles was released in the spring of 1987 and this will make such techniques widely available within the industry. It is also likely that higher resolution laser printers will be on sale before long.

Proceed cautiously, requesting test output wherever you have doubts, but do not be over-timid if you think the process will work for your style of publication. Many newsletters are already successfully published in this way and some books are beginning to appear from DTP originated artwork.

6

Using freelances

Years ago it was quite unusual to find book publishers making regular extensive use of freelances in areas other than illustration and design. In magazines there was a stronger tradition; there freelances were usually writers, often on particular specialist topics, and more run of the mill writing and all editing was under the control of full-time employees.

Now it has become quite normal practice for publishers of both books and magazines to use freelances in every aspect from commissioning through editing to proofreading and design. The reasons are rather interesting.

The most overwhelming one, perhaps, is economy. The cost of staff overheads – what it costs an employer to employ a full-time member of staff – is increasing all the time. Each individual occupies accommodation, he needs somewhere to sit, and something to sit at; he needs lighting, heating, use of a loo and washbasin. National Insurance payments have to be made for him, pension contributions, maybe subsidised lunches, holiday pay, sick pay ... and so on. Every extra full-time member of staff requires time of the administration departments – salary, personnel, etc – necessitating eventually an increase in the number of people who have to be employed to service the others. As employment costs rose, and particularly in the hard times which have faced publishers in recent years, cost cutting exercises highlighted the high price of employing full-time staff.

Meanwhile, the pool of self-employed labour was growing. Experienced staff had been thrown out of work by enforced or voluntary redundancies resulting from the slump in publishing.

Women – a substantial part of the publishing industry – were becoming increasingly reluctant to abandon their careers entirely to become full-time mothers and thought that a combination of work and home would be entirely feasible on a self-employed basis. Young people leaving college with journalism or design qualifications were often unable to find full time work, and were of necessity offering their services on a self-employed basis.

So the market shifted and settled to meet the new state of affairs. Employers have found they can choose the right person for a specific job, pay him an agreed rate and bother no more about where he worked or when, provided the job is completed on time to an acceptable standard. The freelance chooses work that suits him, does it when and where it is convenient and worries no more about commuting or measles . . .

Of course it's not as simple as that. Using freelances successfully with an outcome satisfactory to both parties requires careful thought and preparation on the part of the employer. The financial gain can be considerable but it must be earned by sensible and thoughtful homework. Time spent on such homework is as good as money in the bank and Valium in the bloodstream for without it life can be expensive and fraught indeed.

The Inland Revenue

Anyone who is thinking of employing freelance labour on anything like a regular basis must first be quite clear about the views of the Inland Revenue on the self-employed and those to whom they contract their services. In a nutshell, the Inland Revenue wants its money, and probably the most foolproof way of collecting it is via PAYE. As soon as people become self-employed and start to receive payments from many different sources, it becomes more difficult to monitor their taxable incomes.

The Inland Revenue is increasingly encouraging those who employ freelances to deduct basic rate tax from their payments. Not unnaturally, freelances resent this trend very much. It puts them in the position of having to reclaim from the IR those bits of their payment which were not eligible for tax deduction in the first place, and generally throws their accounts into disorder.

Incidentally, I am discussing here people whose annual

turnover is insufficient for VAT registration. A VAT invoice confers respectability on a freelance. But of course the majority do not earn enough and it is on these people and on those who employ them that the Inland Revenue is becoming increasingly vigilant and tough.

Moreover the IR, being so keen on PAYE, keeps a close eye on *how* freelances are used. If your company is the sole source of revenue for a freelance, or if he or she has a permanent office or even desk in your building, the IR may well try to persuade you that the freelance is, by their reckoning, an employee and must be treated as such: full or part-time, but an employee all the same and subject to PAYE, NI and all those other things . . . and the IR can be very persuasive.

Obviously you may decide that you have a good relationship with your local tax office, and that as you make honest and regular returns of what you pay your suppliers and freelances, then you have discharged your responsibility – it's up to the freelances and the IR to sort out any differences between themselves. Like the customer, the Inland Revenue is always right, so in case of problems later, it is wise to know a few tax facts about your freelances, and to put them down on paper.

And of course you will continue to make regular and accurate returns to the IR about what you have paid each individual. It is often very tempting to pay odd sums for tiny jobs out of petty cash and forget about them. Never be tempted for the sake of expediency and keeping your freelancer happy to conspire with him to defraud the Inland Revenue. It's just not worth it.

Fixed term contracts

If you are looking to employ someone full or part-time on a regular basis for a specified period of time – as you may if you want to fill in for a permanent member of staff on maternity, sabbatical or long-term sick leave – your best bet is to offer a fixed-term contract. This sets down terms and conditions of employment which will prevail until the date specified. You will pay a salary with tax and National Insurance deducted, as you do for regular members of staff, and you can specify other staff benefits to which he is entitled for that period; for example, paid holiday time. At the end of the period he will leave and you will have no further obligation to him in law. However, employment law does state that such an employee who has been with you for more than one year can take action against you for unfair dismissal if he sees fit. After two years he is entitled to redundancy payment if you terminate his employment.

Consecutive fixed term contracts are cumulative; in other words, someone who has been employed on a six month contract from January 1 to June 30 and then for another six months from July 1 until December 31 is deemed under employment law to have been under contract for a year.

Unions

A number of freelance writers, copy editors and proof readers are members of the National Union of Journalists Book or Magazine Branch freelance section. You may have a house agreement with the NUJ which includes clauses governing the payment of such freelances on a casual or regular basis or both.

If for any reason you are proposing to pay a sum which might be thought to fall below the minimum laid down in your house agreement, and even if the freelance is perfectly happy to accept it, beware. You need at the very least a letter setting out terms signed by both parties and you may think it wise to inform the father of your chapel what has been agreed. Clearly that last is up to you and the individual concerned; it would, however, be both foolish and dishonest not to face the fact that people do have second thoughts about the terms they have accepted, and it is easier for them to fight a battle to improve those terms with the strength of a union behind them. Moreover you, in paying below the agreed rate, have reneged on your house agreement, for whatever sensible reasons.

Consultation in advance is almost always more effective than confrontation after an event, in terms of eventual result and in hours wasted and tempers lost and long-term in working relationships with permanent staff.

Make sure in any event that any regular freelance knows of the existence of a chapel at your office and has the name of the father of the chapel.

Why decide to freelance the job?

You may already be in a publishing house where work is routinely put out to freelances. If not, here are some of the reasons you may decide to look for a freelance.

1. If employed staff in one particular section are very busy, you can lighten the load by removing selected and discrete jobs and giving them to someone outside. Examples might include proof reading entire books, designing individual book jackets or magazine covers, copy editing manuscripts.
2. If a particular job comes up regularly but infrequently enough to make employment of someone to do it in-house uneconomic. Examples might include layout of a quarterly magazine, commissioned photography.
3. The need for specialised knowledge not already in-house. Examples might include editing an erudite book in an area new to your company.
4. Filling in for an absent member of staff; i.e. for someone on a known period of maternity, sabbatical or sick leave.
5. To avoid creating an entirely new section of employees to cope with a newly entered field which you are not sure you will continue in.

What to look for and where to look

Here is where what I prefer to call experience, and you may think of as prejudice, shows.

First choice must be from among people you know from your own experience are capable and reliable. In other words, when you decide to put a job out to a freelance, or to bring one into the office to fill a temporary vacancy, think first of all of ex-colleagues who may now, for whatever reason, be self-employed. Don't be too rigid: someone whom you knew as a production editor on a magazine might be just as reliable when faced with a full scale book to copy edit. A feature writer might well jump at the chance of a maternity leave fill-in on the newsdesk.

If no name comes to mind, the next step is to ask around. If you don't know anyone who might do for the job, a colleague might. Recommendation from a colleague is not quite as reliable a reference as your own knowledge, but it is probably the next best thing. If someone does recommend an individual you don't know, ask a few searching questions. Why is he freelancing? What other jobs has he done? Look at them. What other commitments has he?

If it's all hopeless and nobody can come up with a useful name – or all the useful names turn you down – then the NUJ does keep a freelance register which you could consult. There are various agencies which act in the same way as secretarial agencies and may be able to let you have a 'temp'. There are also small companies composed of groups of freelancers who have among their numbers specialists in most publishing areas and will undertake part or all of the production of a book or magazine. Finally, you could advertise in the national or specialist press. *The Guardian*'s media page and *The UK Press Gazette* are both read avidly by many people in the business.

Once you have a name, then the next step is to interview the person concerned. Remember, however anxious you are to find someone, you are the 'customer' and you must like what you are buying. I use the word 'like' advisedly. Of course you must be satisfied that he can and will do a good job, but it's important that you feel you like him. The essence of a happy relationship between freelance and employer is complete two-way communication of both requirements and doubts.

But it is inevitable that if you don't like someone, you tend to hurry and scamp your sessions with him, resulting in incomplete briefing and inadequate work.

It really is worth spending a little time on that first introductory meeting. If there is instant rapport, then you are in the happy position to be able to offer him the job. But if you do have doubts about his ability or his conscientiousness, or whether you are going to be able to get on with him and persuade him to conform to your needs and standards, then think twice before you go ahead. You are perfectly entitled to offer the publishing version of 'don't call us we'll call you', i.e. 'Thank you very much for coming to see me. I'll talk to my colleagues and be in touch very shortly'. You may have wasted a bit of your time – don't feel guilty about wasting his; it's part of the freelance's life not to be offered every job that comes along. Better waste an hour now than weeks of rewriting or re-editing or redesigning later.

What the freelance needs to know from you

1. What he will be paid, when he will be paid, how he will be paid: the amount, gross or net of basic rate of tax. If after the job, how long after, all in one bit or in instalments. What the payment includes (i.e. expenses, incurred or not). Never be shy about talking money. Both you and he have a legitimate interest in getting it straight.
2. The timescale of the job.
3. Who he should ask for in-house if you are not available and he needs help or information.
4. How often you will want to see or hear from him during the course of the job.
5. The names, addresses and phone numbers of other relevant contacts out-house.
6. A complete in depth brief, preferably with the main points written down in advance for him.
7. Samples of similar jobs if they are available.

What you need to know from the freelance

1. What and how he is expecting to be paid.
2. Whether he expects to incur expenses during the course of the job which will be invoiced above the agreed rate, i.e. paper, art materials, travelling to meet authors, film and developing.
3. All addresses and phone numbers at which he is likely to be and when.
4. Whether he is planning to go away for weeks during the course of a job. This may not seem your business, in terms of delivering a complete job at the end of a specified time, but it is sensible to keep tabs on freelances. Murphy's Law translates to mean that they disappear to a country cottage to complete your job in peace two days before an entirely new event occurs which makes it imperative that they come into the office for an update.
5. Whether he is an NUJ (or other union) member.
6. For your peace of mind it might be wise to ascertain (if you don't already know) whether he is also working for your rivals and if so in what capacity.
7. Is he registered as a Schedule D self-employed tax payer? If so, what is his schedule D number?

8. How he expects you to employ him:
   (a) Full time in-house for a fixed term period: you need to draw up a careful contract, for tax and other reasons.
   (b) Regular part-time in-house for a fixed term: you need a careful contract.
   (c) To do one or a number of specific jobs out-house: you need to write a short letter or at least an order form.

The job brief

The freelance should have no surprises from you while a job is in progress. Tell him what you are going to say, say it and then tell him what you have said. There is no such thing as briefing in too much detail. A full, accurate and comprehensible brief is a prerequisite for a satisfactory outcome. This again is something it is worth spending quite a lot of time on. If, and as, you build up a stable of freelances the briefing time will get shorter and shorter as they get to know you and your company and the sorts of books or magazines you publish, but first brief to a newcomer should be a carefully prepared exercise.

What follows is a series of lists and topics to be included in the briefing of freelancers in a number of different areas. If you are searching for someone to do something different, then perhaps you can make up your own list with selected items from some or all of these.

Sub editor to work in-house for a specified period on a magazine

Your verbal briefing must cover the following points, even if some of them are already embodied in a written contract:

1. Terms and conditions of service, i.e hours of work, lunch hours, holiday entitlement if any, money (NUJ rates or not). It is usual to pay freelances a little above equivalent full-time staff to take account of the expenses of self-employment. How he will be paid (in arrears monthly, lump sum ...)
2. Whether the hours are regularly extended by pressure of work (be honest).

3. A short description of the magazine, its policies and the expectations of its readers. Go through an issue, explaining the various sections and where they come from (in-house/out-house contributors etc).

4. A discussion of the production schedule, together with some idea of the volume of copy that will need to be processed day by day. Specify days of particular difficulty (press day for example), and explain how problems are dealt with.

5. An office *Who's Who*, with emphasis on whom the freelance is directly responsible to on a daily basis, and how the hierarchy works. If there is no hierarchy (though there is almost always an informal pecking order at least), identify the person most likely to be helpful in a crisis. Having set the scene, spend time on explaining the type of editing likely to be needed. For example, it is probable that copy written by staff will need less editing work to get it into shape for the typesetters than copy from outside journalists. Most likely to need comprehensive editing is contributed copy from non-professional writers. Everyone knows this, but it is still worth emphasising. Do tell a newcomer if it is your practice to accept and entirely rewrite submitted material.

6. Explain the interface with the design department (if you have one) and indicate where copy editing responsibilities stop and design takes over (marking up typefaces, for example).

7. Tell the freelance if he will be expected to proof-read, collate corrections on galley, check pages, write intros, suggest suitable illustrations.

8. Explain your reference library, what it contains and how to use it.

9. A freelance copy editor should leave the briefing with several copies of the magazine, annotated if that seems helpful, your style sheet, and the design specification if you have one.

Photographer

Before sending a photographer out on a shoot, you should have discussed the following points in some detail:

1. His fees: most photographers charge per day or half day, and will expect you to pay for film, developing and travelling

expenses on top of that. Most professional photographers are VAT registered, so the final account will include VAT at the prevailing rate. Photographers are not cheap. However, most do operate a sliding scale because they understand that less money is available for publishing work than for the much more lucrative advertising photography, and on the whole less for books than for magazines. If you have a budget, then be straight. Say you are unable to pay more than, say, £200 for the photographs, and leave it to the photographer to accept or refuse the assignment. Because freelance photographers are able to set their own fees, they are more likely to accept less lucrative jobs if they see the chance of more work from you later. If this is a carrot you can legitimately dangle, then dangle it.

2. When you want the pictures delivered. You would be wise secretly to advance your schedule a couple of days or more if you can here to allow for slip-ups. If you want the pictures by Friday 13, it does no harm to tell the photographer Monday 9, if that allows him sufficient time to set up and do the job. A photograph in the hand is worth a roll of film jammed in the printing machine.

3. Whether or not he will be doing the job on his own. If you or a colleague are planning to accompany the photographer to 'art direct', he will want to know it.

4. What the job is for: book cover, book illustration, magazine cover, inside the magazine, publicity work, etc; and whether colour or black and white or both.

5. What you are trying to illustrate. If you can give him a copy of the relevant article or chapter, then that will help.

6. Is it to be a studio still life? Who is to provide the articles to be photographed?

7. Will the shot use models? Will they be amateurs (i.e. your colleague at the next desk dressed up as a construction worker) or professionals? If professionals who will choose them? If you do want to use a professional model, ask the photographer's advice. He knows more about that side of the business than you do (probably) and will know which agencies to approach and how to approach them. But remember models are expensive, and you will be billed separately for their time on top of the photography fees. Who will provide the model's clothes and

equipment? If you are expecting the photographer to commission models and act as their dresser on set, then tell him in advance.

8. Is it a location shot? Are you asking the photographer to travel on his own to a bird sanctuary in Suffolk to photograph the rare lesser spotted bustard? If so, who is his contact at the sanctuary? Will you make the arrangements with the contact or should he? Either is acceptable, but it must be clearly understood between you who is doing what, when and to whom. And if you want the bird on its nest, say so now, or you will certainly receive 65 splendid pictures of it diving in the middle of the lake. All this sounds rather like explaining to a four year old, but if your photographer has to leave the Suffolk swamp to telephone you, the chances are that the bustard will have migrated to the Cameroons by the time he gets back to the hide.

9. Spell out the problems. If the sanctuary warden is a testy old fossil, warn the photographer beforehand. If your colleague is a fierce feminist, suggest to the photographer that a lighthearted discussion of his previous nude calendar job is unlikely to relax her for the construction worker shots. The most successful photography comes when there is rapport between artist and subject, and most photographers are adept at creating a good atmosphere if you give them the chance.

10. The photographer should leave the meeting with a copy of the magazine, article or relevant book chapter and a list of contact names.

Out-house copy editor for a book

Your briefing meeting should cover the following topics:

1. Money is an important area of concern to your freelance. The chances are that you will pay a lump sum for the copy editing of a book, and that this will include all expenses (there should be few). The copy editor will work in his own premises, in his own time, and at his own pace within the schedule allowed. He is self-employed, and any expenses he incurs, such as travelling to visit you or to a reference library or purchasing writing materials, are legitimate expenses incurred in business

and can be set against tax when he does his accounts. However, if there are likely to be unusual expenses incurred you may wish to pay them, and this should be made clear at the beginning.

2. The copy editor will need to know whether you have a house style (copy of it for him, please) or whether your aim is simply to have consistency of expression within the book but using the author's preferred method. If the book is part of a series, then clearly he will need the specification for the series, and a copy of any already published volume in the series would be helpful. He will want to know such things as whether paragraphs should be indented, and cross and subheadings annotated. Particularly important in more learned works are instructions as to how references and bibliography are to be presented.

3. The copy editor will wish to know whether he is free to contact the author direct if he has questions or whether all enquiries should be channelled through you or another. Whichever way it is done, all questions should be asked and answered, and the manuscript corrected *before* typesetting.

4. It is worth emphasising (and though it may seem rather patronising, it's worth it for your peace of mind) that if the freelance is finding that very heavy editing is needed or that the manuscript contains wild inaccuracies, he should notify you before proceeding too far. Many publishers now have various forms of escape clause in their contracts and you may wish to consider invoking such a clause early on in the proceedings if the quantity of inaccuracy is such as to throw doubt on the whole value of the book.

5. The other area for which the copy editor should be on the look-out is libel, and while most know this in principle, it is worth spelling out that if they believe they have discovered a libel they should raise it with you quickly, so that legal advice may be sought.

6. Another area which needs careful discussion is time. You must specify quite clearly when the edited manuscript is needed back at the ranch. And it is worth asking the freelance editor to give you warning in advance if for some reason he is going to need an extension. Better to have a couple of weeks' notice of a change in schedule than to discover on delivery day that you cannot move to the next stage. These things do

happen, and everyone in publishing must learn to be flexible if they are to remain in the business.

7. Will you be expecting your copy editor to read proofs too? This will need another explanation of times of expected delivery (both ways), and a polite reminder of the enormous cost of corrections at proof stage.

8. He should leave you with the manuscript, your house style sheet and design specification together with any other relevant books or notes and a list of contact names and numbers.

Proof-reader

1. Once again the discussion of fees is all-important. You will probably choose to pay on a lump sum per manuscript all-in basis.

2. When you specify the date on which you expect to receive the completed work, do try to be realistic. If you leave too little time for proof-reading you will get the quality you deserve.

3. Explain to your proof-reader exactly what he is proof-reading for. Some time ago, when I was doing a little proof-reading, I was surprised to be told to mark only those errors which had happened in typesetting, and to ignore completely those errors which were in the original copy and which had been missed by the copy editor. I simply could not do it and eventually provided a separate list of mistakes of both fact and style. But if you want the equivalent of typesetter's proof-reading, you must say so. Otherwise most readers will correct all errors regardless of where they occurred. If for some reason your proof-reader is checking for typesetting errors only, then perhaps while he is doing it he might as well be asked to note separately any other points which seem dubious.

4. As with the copy editor, the proof-reader needs a copy of the specifications, both for design and style, which you will give him together with the proofs, the original manuscript and a name and telephone number to call in case of enquiries.

Freelance feature writer

A freelance journalist employed to research and write a feature article (or news piece) will expect to be paid the rate as specified by your NUJ house agreement (if you have one) or something close to the going rate currently prevailing in house agreements if you don't have one. You must spell this out and discuss whether travelling or subsistence expenses where these are incurred in the course of preparing the article will be paid on top. If you don't have a house agreement or if the journalist is not a union member (beware this one if the rest of your journalists are) then you should negotiate a fee.

1. Agree the number of words, the payment and the deadline (give yourself a day or two in hand if you can, particularly with freelances you have not used before).
2. Next the freelance will need all the background information you can give him on the topic. Hand over any written information you have: press releases, reports, cuttings, etc, so that he can prepare his questions in advance.
3. If you know of relevant contacts, let him know names and telephone numbers, or tell him where to find them.
4. If the feature requires a visit or two, decide who is to make the arrangements. He may like to have a letter of introduction from the editor of the magazine. Offer him one.
5. If the topic to be covered is a controversial one make sure he understands where the magazine stands: for, against or neutral. If the magazine's policy is likely to be unpopular among the people he needs to contact, warn him in advance, and explain why you have come down on this side of the argument.
6. If any of the contact names you have given your freelance have personal peculiarities, let him know in advance. A certified teetotaller invited out to discuss something over a beer is not going to prove a useful source of information. Most journalists work better if they can strike up a sympathetic bond with the people they are interviewing but if they enjoy controversy, then it is useful to know what to be controversial about.
7. The freelance should leave you carrying copies of your magazine, background information, contact names and telephone numbers.

Following up

However certain you are of your freelance, it is no bad thing to telephone him every now and then to enquire how things are going in a spirit of helpfulness (not mistrust). Unless of course, the job is a short term, out on Monday, back on Friday finished, sort of thing. In that case, telephone calls on Wednesday serve only to annoy.

On anything longer term, particularly for someone you haven't used before, find a plausible reason to ring — something you 'forgot' to mention at the briefing session maybe — just to ask casually how things are going. If the freelance can say that he is well into the job and will have no problem delivering it on time, then your mind will be easier. If he is having problems, a friendly enquiry may encourage him to voice them in time to sort them out. Problems with a job which are presented on the day appointed for delivery as a reason for not delivering are all too common and a great nuisance.

If you are in a position to say 'But I telephoned you last week and you didn't say anything about it', you are also in a position to refuse to pay extra for extra time taken to complete.

Payment

It may seem that I have overstressed the finance aspect of using freelances. But payment is naturally enough an area of paramount importance and it is a pity to lose good people because of payment problems when, with a little early groundwork, most of them can be cured.

I have emphasised throughout the chapter what you should pay, now I want also to emphasise when. In fact, it doesn't matter too much when, so long as you spell it out very clearly in advance to your freelance to give him the opportunity to protest. First, you should specify whether you want your freelance to invoice you or whether receipt of the words or the end of the month or some other trigger will automatically set off the necessary internal administration, eventually resulting in a cheque. Then you should explain just how long that internal adminstration will take. The centralised accounting system now so prevalent often take weeks to come to the point, so it is up to you to tell your freelance that he will receive his cheque six weeks later or whatever.

And incidentally, if you commission 5000 words and then use 1000 of them, you'd better have a watertight reason for only paying for 1000. Shortage of space is not a reason. It simply shows your own lack of foresight. The journalist has done the work and should be paid for it. The only reason for not doing so is that the article is unusable in terms of style or content.

When you do receive an invoice, look at it at once. If you have any doubts about it, it is sensible to raise these at once with the freelance, distasteful and embarrassing though this probably is. It won't go away if you stick it in a drawer. The freelance will follow it up sooner or later, and it's quite difficult to demand a reduction weeks after the event. If you have any reason to dispute the bill, gather the evidence on to your desk and then do it straightaway. In fact, you should have already told the freelance that the work was not up to standard when he delivered it, or as soon as was feasible afterwards, so your refusal to agree the invoice should not come as a surprise. As I said earlier, nothing should come as a surprise, least of all a payment problem.

Here, as a very rough guide, are the sorts of rates prevailing in 1987. Please understand that no rates are fixed and that NUJ or other house agreements override them.

Photography	from £200/day upwards + expenses (can be much more)
Out-house news/feature writing	£80–£100/1000 words + some expenses
In-house casual journalism	between 1.3 and 1.7 × equivalent staff rate
Book proof-reading	£75–£100/manuscript or £6–£7/hour
Design	from £15/hour upwards (can be much more)
Book copy editing	rate per book, depending on length and complexity or £7–£10/hour

Ten commandments of using freelances

DO	talk money unambiguously.
DO	emphasise delivery dates.
DO	put long term or multi-job agreements in writing.
DO	brief fully.
DO	keep in touch if the job is to take some time.
DON'T	use somebody new without investigating his ability in advance.
DON'T	overestimate freelancer's knowledge of your organisation/job.
DON'T	disguise/ignore possible difficulties.
DON'T	accept shoddy work. Be brave and say it is no good.
DON'T	pay out of petty cash.

7

Preparing advertising copy

Few publishing companies have departments specifically to prepare advertising copy and it often falls to the lot of the copy editor to tackle this really quite critical stage in the publishing process. I hope this chapter provides a few useful guidelines.

Advertising your own books and magazines

In this section I assume that you intend to prepare your own advertisements without the help of an advertising agency – though if you do use an agency it may still be helpful in suggesting the services you should expect them to perform for you.

An advertising campaign, however, small, should go through five distinct phases:

Planning and budgeting
Media planning
Copy preparation
Publication of advertisement(s)
Follow up

In order that the copy does what it is intended to do, it's useful to have some idea of the surrounding phases.

Planning and budgeting

The most important part of any campaign plan is to decide what you want to get out of it. And obvious though this may seem when you see it written down, nevertheless, many, many advertising campaigns are embarked on by people who have no clear, ultimate goal. They are thus unable to analyse their results properly in order to do better next time.

Once you have an aim in view, then you can most sensibly plan how to reach it and see later where you went wrong ... or why you got it right.

So what are you hoping to achieve?

Sales of an individual book or series?
Wider exposure of the company as an important publisher in a particular area of interest?
Both these things?
High sales of a particular issue of a magazine?
Higher sales of a magazine on a long-term basis?
    on the bookstalls?
    by subscription?
    both?
Wider awareness of a number of your magazines?

All these aims require a different approach in terms both of copy and medium. Beware of trying to do too much at once. Portmanteau advertisements tend to lack impact and you often achieve more by concentrating on a single area of concern.

Once you have decided on your main aim (you may of course also achieve some of the others in passing) you can begin to decide how best to reach it.

First, how much money do you have to spend? You probably already have a budget fixed but if not it is wise to fix one for yourself. Open-ended budgets are a dangerous temptation. It is best to attempt the most cost-effective plan you can devise within tight financial constraints, opening out your spending only if you and your colleagues are convinced that the returns on extra expenditure are certainly worthwhile. I cannot, however, give much help as to what your budget should be; you know best what your market will need.

Once you know what you have to spend and what you want to achieve, you are ready to decide what to do. The promotion of any product may take a number of forms. But we are concerned here with copy preparation, so I assume that you have decided that the best way to reach your target is by conventional ink-on-paper advertising.

Media planning

Now comes the time to decide where and how you are going to advertise your product.

If you intend to advertise in the press – in other words, if you are trying to reach an audience of relatively unknown people – then your first step must be to define your target audience. You may of course have concluded that your target audience is so well known to you that your best plan is to subject them to ordeal by mailshot, in which case you can skip this section and move to the next.

Who are the people you are trying to reach: the general public, librarians, bookshops, special interest groups? Do they buy on impulse, regularly, by recommendation? Are your potential buyers already aware of your product in a general way or will it be entirely new to them?

All these factors and more will influence your choice of advertising medium and the wording and design of the copy.

Once the nature of your target audience is as clear as you can make it, and you have decided what your advertising campaign is designed to encourage them to do *and* you know how much you can afford to spend, your objective might be described as moving the maximum number of the target audience through this decision-making process:

Ignorance/apathy
Awareness
Interest
Desire
Action

Now you must consider the merits of the various publications available to you. In producing a schedule of advertisements which will have the maximum impact for the agreed cost, a number of points must be taken into account.

First you should select a general group which apparently have an appropriate target audience:

National press
Regional newspapers
Local newspapers
Consumer magazines
Professional and trade magazines
Special interest magazines, etc.

Having decided on a group (or more than one) for the advertisements, you should go on to look more closely at the individual publications within that group, examining the readership profile for such indications as circulation (ABC or publisher's statement), age of readers, gender, social class, buying habits, magazine life and pass-on rates.

Naturally not all these factors need always be considered, but for a general interest book to be advertised in consumer magazines, for example, such details are important if the advertisement is to reach the audience for which it is intended.

Media planners in the agencies have access to masses of information on the many thousands of magazines and newspapers published in the UK. Some have computer links to a databank service; others have micros plus software which enable them to produce advertising schedules optimising the various combinations of desirable elements offered by the media. You can do the same things yourself: a series of telephone calls to those magazines or newspapers deemed most suitable will bring in the post the available information: readership profiles, page rates, special offers and so on, together with the production details which will be needed for the stage of copy preparation.

Next you should consider how you believe the greatest impact might be made. How many advertisements, in how many magazines? All at the same time, at regular intervals, or in short bursts with gaps between? How large? In colour or black and white? There are no hard and fast rules. Experience, guesswork, the schedules of your competitors, will all help you.

Thus mathematical computation or a combination of experience and best-guesswork will eventually provide you with a media schedule. The space must be booked in the various magazines and papers and you can move on to the next processes – preparing the copy and designing the advertisements – tasks which should, but so often don't, go hand in hand.

Copy preparation

Everyone involved in preparing an advertisement for publication should know, from the beginning, where it is to go (which magazine, and whether in a special position), whether mono or four colour, the exact page or part-page size (text and bleed), how the copy is to be presented (artwork, colour separations etc.) *and* the copy date.

Ideally copywriter and designer will be briefed, together, in sufficient time for them to come up with a punchy, informative advertisement, carefully matched to the magazine in which it will appear, the audience it is intended for, and the other advertisements/promotional activities for the product. More realistically, the briefing will probably be piecemeal and the time between it and the copy date too short. However, for the advertisement to be any use at all, the copywriter and designer must know all these details and have an idea of the overall coverage of the advertisement campaign.

If you are planning to run the same advertisement in a number of different magazines or newspapers, then it must be written and designed in such a way as to appeal to the widest possible audience and include all relevant details. Separate advertisements for separate audiences which may in some instances overlap should be written in different styles but might perhaps have an overall 'look'.

Advertisements which include an order form of any sort must be coded (on the form itself) so that the response you receive from different advertisements can later be analysed. If there is no order form you might consider a code (which changes with each advertisement) within your address, so that you can monitor response rates from different magazines, e.g. Dept A1, A2, and so on.

Returned order forms can sometimes form the basis of a useful mailing list for later publications, so you might also consider including a request for other information (e.g. professional status) on your order form.

Another method of inviting readers' response, much used in trade and technical publications, is the use of the reader service card. Your advertisement will include a number, inserted by the periodical concerned, and interested readers are invited to mark the corresponding number on a pre-paid postcard inserted in the periodical. Such enquiries are then passed to the advertiser.

Whether you are copywriting an advertisement or merely checking and marking up someone else's copy, you should ensure that all the relevant information has been included and that the advertisement is suitable in tone for the medium in which it is to appear. Check the inclusion of:

> Title and author
> Price
> Publisher (Logo?)
> Where/when available

If the plan is to repeat the same advertisement a number of times over a period of months, it's also worth checking that it does not contain copy which will become outdated during its run. This may seem a trivial point but phrases like 'next month' or even 'next year' can slip through to mislead the reader.

What follows are some very simple examples of the way advertisement copy can be changed to fit the publication in which it is to appear. The message is nonetheless true for having been made unsubtly. To have impact, an advertisement must be appropriate to the audience and to the medium.

EXAMPLE 1: THREE APPROACHES TO ADVERTISING A NEW BOOK

> When In Doubt, STRIKE OUT
> The autobiography of a chief sub editor
> By Jill Baker
> Deanland Publishers Ltd
> £9.95 hardback
> Publication: August 1 1987

The advertising schedule for this book is as follows:

1. Half page black and white ad in *The Bookseller* July 1 1987 (*trade press*)
2. 90cm × 2 columns black and white ad in the *Sunday Times*, September 3 1987 (*consumer press*)
3. Quarter page black and white in *UK Press Gazette* September 3 1987 (*professional press*)

All the advertisements are fairly economical in scale. It is assumed that the book is not going to be a run-away best seller; on the other hand, it has a sufficiently wide appeal to make consumer-press advertising worthwhile.

The Bookseller

When in Doubt, STRIKE OUT
Jill Baker   (Photograph of jacket)

A sizzling story of malice and intrigue behind the decorous covers of a professional journal. The author of HOW TO SWIM WITH SHARKS describes with wit and insight her battle to maintain the integrity of a magazine under siege by the forces of big business.
Another winner from Deanland Publishers, Cowley Road, Cambridge, telex 0371845, 24-hour ordering service 0223 851534.

Cover price £9.95 hardback
Publication date: August 1 1987
* See the author on Parkinson, August 10 1987 (Flash)

The Sunday Times

When in Doubt STRIKE OUT
Jill Baker   (Photograph of jacket)

An experienced magazine journalist explains with wit and insight who really controls what we read – and why. If you thought there was no censorship in Britain, Jill Baker will make you think again.

'Compulsive . . .' The Listener

Deanland Publishers
£9.95

The UK Press Gazette

When in Doubt STRIKE OUT

Jill Baker   (Photograph of jacket)

Journalists who have experienced the conflict between open reporting and financial interests in the newspaper industry will welcome Jill Baker's exposé of how big business controls our press. The author was editor of a leading weekly magazine for ten fighting years and her analysis of what is wrong with our industry is stunning in its frankness.

Deanland Publishers
£9.95 hardback

Notes

The Bookseller: Trade press announcement. Includes a picture of the book jacket, with the title clearly visible; this is to provide visual recognition when the publishers' rep comes along to sell the book. The copy also includes some emotive words (sizzling, malice), the title of the author's previous book (which sold well; if it had been a flop, we wouldn't have mentioned it), the publication date, the price and the name and address and telex and teleordering service number of the publisher. A flash or star mentions a TV appearance; any outside publicity which may help to bring in the buying public must be included in a trade advertisement.

The Sunday Times: Quality consumer press. The Sunday Times has a reputation for crusading, hence the copyline on censorship. An extract from a review in a reputable magazine is a good selling point, as those who read the review pages are 'thinking' book buyers. No mention of the publication date as the book is, we hope, freely available at booksellers by now. The TV appearance is over and in any event, irrelevant in this advertisement.

UK Press Gazette: In the weekly professional magazine for journalists the copy seeks to identify with the interests of the readers once again, in a slightly different approach. The underlying message is that we all know what goes on; here is someone brave enough to speak out, and there is perhaps a hint that she skates titillatingly along the edge of libel.

These examples, or rather the points they make, are just as valid for advertising magazines. In other words, you might choose to highlight specific areas of interest covered by the magazine in separate advertisements, aimed at different parts of the readership. Or you might prefer to prepare one catch-all advertisement for insertion into one or a number of publications, intended either to direct readers towards a specific issue, or to remind potential readers of its existence and to boost the loyalty of its regulars.

By substituting copy B for copy A, the following advertisement could be made to serve either purpose. Ideally it would be designed to reflect the image of the magazine, and would probably include a photograph of the current cover, or several covers.

EXAMPLE 2: ADVERTISING A MAGAZINE

One steadfast element remains in these uncertain times:
MAJESTY
For all who love our Queen and Country
Either A. Forthcoming issues will include: *or*
B. The May issue includes:
* *Top of the Class*
  Prince William's teacher reveals his amazing progress
* *Keeper of the Queen's Horse*
  His daily life in words and pictures
* *WIN a Holiday for Two*
  and visit the stately homes of England
Monthly from your newsagent, price 75p.

Notes

The headline is deliberately ambiguous; is it the Royal Family or the magazine which is steadfast? No matter – the word is emotive in itself, and the wording suitably pompous as is the subheading beneath the title of the magazine.

The articles listed are chosen to appeal to the widest possible audience – royal children and animals and a hint of pictures. Together with the opportunity of something for nothing, these should prove a winning combination. Nobody is interested in who publishes a magazine, but they do want to know where to get it and how much it will set them back...

Follow up

Unless you are able to analyse the results of your advertising campaign, at least to some extent, you will not be able to improve for the next one.

At its very simplest level, analysis might take the form of each individual involved in the campaign considering his part and wondering whether he might have done it better. This may be something you do as a matter of course with every piece of work in which you are involved – it is certainly a good discipline. You might then consider whether the advertisements work as a whole, and if not why not. If this is as far as you go, then you will at least have learned something for next time.

More usefully, you might look at the sales analysis for the book or magazine concerned, to compare the dates of sales highpoints with the dates your advertisements appeared. If there seems to be a relationship, then you may be able to draw some conclusions about the relative effectiveness of advertisements in different periodicals.

If your advertisements carried a coded order form, then you will also be able to compare the relative effectiveness of the media you chose. If your code was part of the address, make sure that the envelopes containing the forms are retained for analysis.

If your order forms included other information about the respondents this too can be analysed and retained for future use. If you do this by computer, don't forget that the Data Protection Act requires you to register as a holder of such information.

If your advertisement was included in a reader service card scheme, then you will eventually receive a set of cards on which your number has been indicated. These readers want further information about your book or magazine, and their names too might usefully form part of a mailing list for the future.

However brief or intensive your analysis, don't omit it altogether.

Mailshots

If you can obtain a list of names and addresses of people you believe will be particularly interested in your publication, then a targetted mailshot is often very worthwhile. Untargetted mailshots are probably best kept for consumer goods.

A mailshot often consists simply of a letter addressed individually by name or by suitable appellation, (e.g. 'Dear Colleague' or 'Dear Angler'). Name is obviously best if you can manage it. The letter will go on to direct the reader's attention to your publication, giving all the details and the reasons why he should want to buy it. You may want to include an incentive: a pre-publication discount, a small free gift, or the opportunity of buying two years' subscription for the price of one. Many people affect to despise such devices but there is no doubt that they do work if they are carefully matched to the prospective readership.

Mailshot letters have a style of their own, with which we have all been given rather too much opportunity to become familiar. But here are just a few tips:

1. Don't make it too long. You will lose your reader's interest if he has to turn the page.
2. Make it look easy to read. A tightly packed page of single spaced typing is uninviting. Remember you are competing with a lot of other post for your reader's attention.
3. Match the style to the publication. The popular chatty style of so many consumer mailshots is not suitable for serious volumes and if overdone may serve to alienate the reader who will identify the letter with the product.
4. Give the reader as little as possible to do if he does decide to answer your mailshot. A separate order form with clear instructions about payment included on it, rather than in the body of the letter, plus a Freepost address, or a reply paid envelope, will encourage your reader to reply. If he has to read your letter again to find out where to send his order or search for a stamp to put on it, he may well forget or decide not to bother.

You may prefer to send a brochure or catalogue rather than or together with a letter. All the same points apply.

If this method of advertising is new to you, you might consider dividing your list of addresses in half and trying different letters to the two halves, or a letter to one group and a brochure to the other. Comparing the responses to different forms of approach is a useful exercise for the future.

Advertisements in your publication

Without the revenue generated by advertisements many – most – magazines would not be viable. Certain types of books, too (for example, directories, catalogues and certain handbooks) also rely on advertisement revenue to subsidise the cover price and provide a profit.

It is vital that advertisement processing is a slick and efficient operation leaving as few openings for gremlins as possible.

You will, of course, have prepared, printed and distributed as widely as possible among your clients an advertising rates and data sheet. We are not here concerned with rates, but it is obviously very important that the data is correct, umambiguous and complete.

A data sheet which gives all the necessary production details and copy dates should ensure that perhaps 90 per cent of advertisements submitted to you by your clients are suitable and in time for inclusion in the magazine or book. Once their acceptability is established they need only be entered in your system and passed to the next stage.

The other 10 per cent will be the wrong size, incorrectly prepared or late and it is these few which cause disproportionate heartache. So it is sensible that you have some clearly understood rules for dealing with the problems which will inevitably occur.

Obviously, you will want to do your best to include all booked advertisements, so your processing system should include an automatic tripwire which alerts someone that the copy or artwork for a booked advertisement has not arrived, in sufficient time for the client to be warned that the deadline is near.

If deadline time comes and nothing has been received, it must be very clear exactly when a decision to omit the advertisement has to be made. And just whose decision it is. To hold up production for a single advertiser may be too costly in terms of both money and lost goodwill from all the others!

Your system should include ways of spotting incorrectly prepared artwork and then for correcting it, and for charging your clients for corrections made by you. All advertisements received from other people for publication by you should be examined for suitability *at the time of receipt*. Press day is not the time to discover that they are unacceptable in terms of production or content.

There should be no doubt about what is acceptable content, incidentally. Some periodicals will not accept cigarette advertisements or advertisements for abortion agencies or advertisements for homosexual clubs. It is usually the editor who feels strongly about these things. If there is no established policy about acceptability and you feel in doubt, raise the alarm early. A reasonable discussion in plenty of time is always better than a last minute panic to fill the space left by an advertisement which has been pulled out, or – worse – an after-publication shouting match along the lines of 'you should have known better!'

If your periodical contains a reader enquiry card, do remember to include an appropriate number on each of the advertisements.

Most display advertisements – in other words those referring to products of one kind or another – will come 'ready made'. But if they do arrive as marked up copy, do ensure before you send them for typesetting that the typefaces chosen by the advertiser are held by your typesetter and that the words will fit into the booked space. Copy which arrives without typefaces marked can be designed by you. In either case you should send the advertiser a proof for correction, specifying on it the latest date that corrections can be made.

Classified advertising is likely to arrive as copy. Most periodicals which carry classified advertising have established a group of three or four different styles in which such advertising can be set out: single or double column, capitals or lower case, bold or roman type, or combinations of these. The advertiser chooses the style he prefers, and the periodical's typesetter sets the copy in that style.

When the copy arrives it should be quickly checked for acceptability, correctness (spelling and so on) and legibility. It must be marked with the chosen style (often denoted by 'style A, B', etc), identified in some way (perhaps simply numbers) and roughly cast off. If the classified advertising is divided into sections, then the section must be given. Classified advertising may constitute a large part of the magazine and is of necessity often the last part to go to press. There will be little time, if any, for proof reading or second thoughts, so it is important that the copy is correct and easily read by the typesetter. And that instructions are complete.

You should keep a running total of the space needed by the classified advertisements, together with a note of what they are (or more simply, how many). You can then check at a later stage that all have been included, simply by counting them.

Finally, and once again, you must be very clear when the deadline for accepting copy is. Deadlines are made to be broken – occasionally – but regular overrunning will eventually lead to something going seriously wrong, at the typesetter, at the printer or perhaps within your own organisation. Wherever it is, everyone will suffer. If you see disaster looming, push the panic button early. With goodwill and cooperation, frightful situations can be retrieved. But if you try to cover up or blindly hope that all will be well, you may find yourself without a magazine – and perhaps without a job.

The ten commandments for preparing successful advertising

DO	clarify what you hope to achieve
DO	fit the message to the medium
DO	double-check that all relevant details are included
DO	make response easy
DO	analyse your results
DON'T	expect any publication to sell itself
DON'T	devise a campaign piecemeal
DON'T	rely on guesswork when research can be done
DON'T	leave everything to the last minute
DON'T	miss copy dates

Further reading

BARLOW, Geoff (1987). *Typesetting and Composition*, Blueprint Publishing.

BARRASS, Robert (1978). *Scientists Must Write: A Guide to Better Writing for Scientists, Engineers and Students*, Chapman and Hall.

BUTCHER, Judith (1981). *Copy Editing: The Cambridge Handbook*, Cambridge University Press.

CARD, Michael (1987). *Interfacing Word Processors and Phototypesetters*, Blueprint Publishing.

CAVENDISH, J. M. (1974). *A Handbook of Copyright in British Publishing Practice*, Cassell.

CUTTS, Martin (1980). *Writing Plain English: Why It Should Be Done; How It's Been Done; How You Can Do It*, Plain English Campaign.

EVANS, H. *Editing and Design: A Five Volume Manual of English Typography and Layout*, 1. *Newsman's English*; 2. *Handling Newspaper Text*; 3. *News Headlines*; 4. *Pictures on a Page*; 5. *Newspaper Design*, Heinemann for the National Council for the Training of Journalists.

EVANS, H., EVANS, M. and NELKI, A. (1979). *The Picture Researchers' Handbook*, David and Charles.

EVANS, Harold, (1983). *Good Times, Bad Times*, Weidenfeld and Nicholson.

GRIMOND, John (1986). *The Economist Pocket Style Book*, The Economist.

HARRISON, Nancy (1985). *Writing English: A Users' Manual*, Croom Helm.

INSTITUTE OF SCIENTIFIC AND TECHNICAL COMMUNICATORS (1986). *ISTC Handbook of Technical Writing and Publication Techniques*, Heinemann.

MUMBY, F. A. and NORRIE, I. (1974). *Publishing and Bookselling*, fifth edition, Jonathan Cape.

O'CONNOR, M. and WOODFORD, F. P. (1978). *Writing Scientific Papers in English*, Pitman Medical.

PEACOCK, J., BERRILL, C. and BARNARD, M. (1986). *The Print and Production Manual*, Blueprint Publishing.

PTT (1985). *Periodical Journalism: A Guide to Editorial Practice*, PTT.

ROGERS, Geoffrey (1986). *Editing for Print*, Macdonald.

SELLERS, Leslie (1968). *Doing it in Style*, Pergamon Press.

—— (1968). *The Simple Subs Book*, Pergamon Press.

Glossary

AA **Author's Alteration** See **author's corrections.**

accents Marks added to letters in some languages to indicate stress, e.g. é (acute e) in French.

access The ability to retrieve data from a computer storage medium or peripheral device.

acetate Transparent sheet of film fixed over camera-ready artwork used for positioning repro or for marking instructions.

acoustic coupler A device to which a telephone can be attached and which transmits data over phone lines from one computer to another.

addendum Late addition to book after printing, often as a pasted-in slip.

address The character or string of characters identifying a unique storage location in computer memory or backing store.

advance feed Sprocket holes in paper tape which align with code hole positions to indicate start of tape.

agate Obsolete term for 5½pt type. Also called **ruby.** Standard measurement of advertising columns: 14 agate lines=1 column inch.

algorithm An arithmetical computer routine in the form of programmed instructions which performs a recurring task.

align To line-up type, horizontally or vertically, e.g. **base alignment.**

allotter Computer device which directs files to specific peripherals.

alphabet 1. An ordered set of letters or symbols and associated marks used in a **language.** 2. A set of types of one particular kind, e.g. roman lower case or italic capitals of a specific design and size.

alphabet length Length of a lower-case type font.

alphanumeric Relating to the full alphabetic and numeric character set of a machine.

ampersand Symbol & for the word 'and'.

analog computer A computer which represents numerical values by analogous physical variables such as speed, length or voltage rather than by digital representation. Contrast **digital computer.**

appearing size The physical size of a type, as opposed to its nominal point size. Two typefaces of the same point size can have very different appearing sizes.

appendix Addition to a book or document following the main text.

applications software Programs which are applied to solve specific problems, such as business systems.

arabic figures The numerals 1, 2, 3, 4, etc., as distinguished from the Roman I, II, III, IV. Evolved from Arabic symbols.

archive To store data economically off-line for future use in a computer system.

area make-up Bringing together text and graphics into a page or area layout.

area storage A buffer of storage reserved for 'live' data en route between a peripheral and its storage destination in a computer.

arithmetic unit Computer unit which performs calculations.

art See **artwork.**

art paper Paper coated with china clay and polished to a high finish.

artwork Original illustrative copy or typesetting ready for reproduction at pre-film stage.

Artype Proprietary name for a make of **transfer type.**

ascender The part of a lower-case character which extends above the **x-height.** As in 'b', 'd', 'f', etc. See also **descender.**

ASCII American Standard Code for Information Interchange. The most widely used data transmission code for computers. It comprises 7 or 8 information bits and one parity bit for error checking. Used by most word processors and the IBM PC and compatibles but not by IBM mainframes, which transmit in **EBCDIC.**

ASPIC Author's Standard Pre-press Interfacing Code. System of typographic text coding developed by the Electronic Village typesetting company and adopted by the British Printing Industries Federation as an industry standard of electronic mark-up. See also **SETM, SGML** and **generic coding.**

ASR Answer Send and Receive. Machine which can send to and receive from a computer by paper tape.

assembler A computer program which translates a symbolic language into **machine code.** See also **assembly language.**

assembler box Part of a Linotype composing machine in which the line is assembled.

assembly To bring together pieces of film or paper to make up lines or pages.

assembly language A computer language close to **machine code** which needs an **assembler** to translate.

asterisk Star-shaped symbol (*) often used as a footnote reference mark.

asynchronous transmission Method of data transmission in which each unit of data is delimited by a start and stop bit.

author's corrections Corrections made by the author on proofs to the original copy, as distinct from **literals** made by the typesetter.

author's proof Corrected proof sent to the author for approval.

auto-kerning See **kern, kerning.**

automatic heading The positioning of a heading on consecutive pages by means of an instruction on the pagination set-up program.

auto-reversal film Type of film used for duplication which does not require a second stage of contacting. Used to reverse image on film.

auxiliary storage See **backing store.**

a/w See **artwork.**

azerty Alternative to the standard **QWERTY** keyboard arrangement of characters, in use in Europe and accommodating **accents.**

background Computer-processing mode which can occur concurrently with the main use of the machine, e.g. hyphenation and justification of a text file while other material is being input.

backing store Mass storage medium on a computer, e.g. floppy disk, magnetic tape, etc.

back margin The margin of a book nearest the spine.

back number Copy of a previous issue of a periodical.

backslant Backward sloping typeface, i.e. opposite to italic.

back up Extra standby equipment, personnel or copies of data.

bad break Undesirable end-of-line hyphenation of a word.

bar code Symbol representing a unique product code, presented in standardised machine-readable form and appearing on the outside of a publication for stock control purposes.

baryta Special type of coated paper sometimes used for reproduction proofs.

base alignment Method of aligning characters, e.g. of different sizes, so that they appear to stand on the same base line.

base line Horizontal line on which characters in a line of type appear to stand.

BASIC Beginners All-purpose Symbolic Instruction Code. A widely used high-level computer-programming language.

batch Method of computer processing where input data is collected into batches before processing, as distinct from **real time,** or **interactive.**

batter Broken or damaged type, blocks or plates.

baud Number of computer bits transmitted per second over a data-communications channel.

beard Distance from the bottom of the **x-height** of a piece of metal type to the bottom edge of the body.

bed The flat metal part of a printing machine which holds the type forme during printing.

bell code Code permitting more phototypesetting commands than is normal in a six-channel coding structure.

bf bold face.

bi-directional printing Movement both from left to right and right to left in a line-printer machine (e.g. daisy-wheel printer) thus increasing output (conventional printers move only left to right).

binary Numbering system using the base 2 as opposed to decimal which uses the base 10. The only digits used are 0 and 1. See also **bit.**

bit 'Binary information transfer' or 'binary digit' is the basic information unit in computer systems. Each bit is either 0 or 1. A group of 8 bits is known as a **byte,** and defines one character.

bitmap An assembly of **pixels** which describe an image, either as display on screen or as output to an **imagesetter.**

black and white Single-colour black only originals or reproductions as distinguished from multicolour. Sometimes called **mono** or **monochrome.**

black box Colloquial term for an electronic device which converts one type of input into another form of output. See also **code converter, media converter, multi-disk reader.**

black letter Also called **gothic.** A type style based upon a formal manuscript hand of the fifteenth century.

blad Sample pages of a book produced in the form of a booklet and used for promotional purposes.

blind keyboard Typesetting keyboard with no visual display (e.g. screen or marching display) or hard copy of keying.

block 1. Letterpress printing surface (made from etched metal) for printing illustrations. 2. Computer term for a group of **bytes** of information.

blueprints Contact dyeline proofs made on paper from film. Used for general checking purposes especially positioning. Also called **blues** (USA), **diazo** prints and **ozalid** prints.

body 1. Metal composing term for the solid metal of a piece of type carrying the printing surface. 2. Phototypesetting term for the size of the body of type, e.g. 12pt=a 12pt body.

body matter Text pages as distinct from prelims, index, display, etc.

body size Same as typesetting term **body.**

bold Heavier version of a typeface, as distinct from light or medium. Sometimes abbreviated to **bf** (bold face).

book proof Page proofs paperback-bound in the form of the finished book.

borders Decorative designs usually edging the page or type.

BOT Beginning of tape. Mark showing start point of computer tape.

bourgeois Obsolete term for 9pt type.

bowl Typographical descriptive term for enclosed part of a letter as in a 'p' or 'o'.

boxhead ruling Space at head of a ruled column where headings are to be inserted.

BPIF British Printing Industries Federation.

brace Form of bracket, mainly used in tables.

brackets Pair of marks [], used for editorial notes in text. See **parentheses.** 2. In typographic design, refers to the small curve or cup where a serif joins the letter stem.

BRAD Acronym for British Rate and Data. Publication listing all UK publications and their advertising specifications and requirements.

branch A point in a computer program where one of a set of alternatives is chosen by the computer according to its instructions.

brevier Obsolete type size, approximately 8pt.

brilliant Obsolete term for 4pt type.

British Standards Institution British national co-ordinating body for technical standards in industry.

bromide Photographic light-sensitive paper used in photographic reproduction or phototypesetting, producing a positive image.

brownprint Also known as Van Dyke or brownline. Term (mainly used in America) for a photographic print from a negative used to check positioning before making printing plates. Similar to **blueprint.**

BSI British Standards Institution.

bubble memory Form of backing storage which uses magnetically charged crystal chips to hold data. Not widely used.

buffer Computer storage used when information needs to be held temporarily en route from one device to another.

bug Computer term for a defect interfering with a computer operation.

bullet Phototypesetting term for a large dot used for ornamentation.

byte The smallest addressable unit of computer storage, usually comprising 8 bits. Equivalent to one character.

c&sc Capitals and small capitals, i.e. words which begin with capitals and have the other characters in small caps the height of the lower-case body size.

calligraphy Art of handwriting or script drawing.

camera-ready artwork or **camera-ready copy (CRC)** or **camera-ready paste-up (CRPU)** Typematter or type and line artwork pasted up into position ready for photographing.

canon Obsolete term for 48pt type.

cap height The height of the capital letters of a font.

caps Capitals. Upper-case letters, e.g. A, B, C, etc. See also **lower-case.**

caption Text accompanying and describing an illustration.

card punch Keyboard machine which perforates cards for data storage or input. A **card reader** reads the data.

carding Thin spacing of lines of type using strips of card instead of lead. See **leading.**

caret Proofreader's mark indicating an insertion.

carriage return Keyboard command key which terminates a line of setting and may enter text from a computer screen into memory.

cartridge disk Computer storage disk enclosed in a plastic case.

case Partitioned tray containing type for hand composition. See also **lower case** and **upper case.**

cassette Small reel-to-reel tape holder for audio or data recording.

casting 1. The process of forcing molten metal into a mould to create a character or slug of type. 2. Producing **stereotypes** from **mats** in newspaper printing. A **casting box** is used for this purpose.

casting off Calculating the number of pages a given amount of copy will make when set in a given typeface and size to a given area.

catch line A temporary heading on a manuscript or proof for identification.

cathode ray tube See **CRT.**

CCD Charge Coupled Device. A semiconductor that contains a row of image sensing elements or 'photosites'. The light energy which falls on these phorosites generates a charge proportional to the light energy and the resulting signals can then be controlled and monitored.

CD-ROM Compact Disk Read Only Memory. Pre-recorded non-erasable digital data disk, used successfully for the storage of large amounts of standard information. See **optical disk, optical digital disk.**

central processing unit See **CPU.**

centre To position type centrally in a given measure.

centre-feed Paper-tape sprocket holes that line up with the middle of code holes. See also **advance feed.**

centre notes Notes placed between columns of a page.

chad The waste punched out of paper tape or cards.

channel 1. Electrical path of a data stream. 2. Row of holes in punched tape.

chapel Smallest unit of a print union's departmental or company grouping. **Father of chapel** or **Mother of chapel** is the elected chairperson.

chapter head Chapter title and/or number.

character Letter, figure or symbol of type.

character count Total number of characters and spaces in a piece of copy.

character printer A printer which prints individual characters as distinct from complete lines. Often capable of reproducing specific typefaces.

character recognition Reading characters by machine, often for digital storage.

character set The full range of characters in memory on a keyboard, or available for output from a machine.

chase Rectangular steel frame in which type and blocks are locked up for letterpress printing.

check digit An extra digit calculated automatically from other digits in a data item and used to check its accuracy.

chip A small electronic component containing extensive logic circuits.

cicero European 12pt unit of type measure. Equal to 4.511mm.

circulating matrix The Linotype matrix from which type is cast.

classified Advertisements for job vacancies, articles for sale, etc., set in columns and sorted by classification.

clean line An electrical power line dedicated to one machine and therefore not subject to **spiking.**

clean proof A printer's proof in which there are no errors.

clean tape Computer tape with no data on it or with all unnecessary codes removed.

clear To empty memory (on a screen, a file, etc.).

close up Reduce spacing between characters of type or other elements on a proof.

cluster A group of items of equipment located together.

COBOL Common Business-Oriented Language. High-level computer programming language widely used in commercial data processing.

code A character-string or line of symbolic instructions to a computer.

code converter A device which converts one set of symbolic codes into another.

code structure The structure scheme of a symbolic code.

cold composition Any typesetting method which does not use hot metal typecasting.

colophon A printer's or publisher's identifying symbol, printed on spines and title pages.

'colour' The lighter or darker appearance of a piece of typeset text, created by the combination of typeface, size and interlinear space specified.

colour split Facility of a composition system to output on separate pages of bromide or film, copy which has been flagged for printing in different colours.

column inch A newspaper measure of text space, one column wide and one inch deep.

command A computer instruction specifying an operation.

communications The electronic transfer of data between different hardware.

comp 1. To **compose**. 2. A **compositor**. 3. A **comprehensive**: a layout showing everything in position.

compact disk See **CD-ROM**.

compatibility The ability of two pieces of electronic hardware to emulate each other and to communicate with each other.

compiler A computer program which converts programs from a 'high-level' language to a language understandable by the machine such as BASIC, COBOL, FORTRAN.

compose To make up type into lines and/or pages. The operator is called a **compositor**.

composing stick A hand-held, adjustable tray in which a compositor sets type by hand.

composition sizes Types under 14pt in size, i.e. originally those sizes in hot metal which could be set by a mechanical composition caster. As distinct from **display sizes**.

computer typesetting The use of a computer to store and display typesetting and to perform many other functions such as hyphenation and justification.

concurrent processing The execution of two programs simultaneously.

condensed type A typeface with characters narrower in set than the standard face of the typeface family.

configuration The arrangement of peripherals into a computer system.

console The keyboard which controls the operations of a mainframe computer.

contact print A photographic print of a negative or positive made in contact with, and therefore the same size as, the original.

contact screen Halftone screen used in direct contact with the photographic film for creating halftones.

contents page Page of a book or magazine explaining the contents and where they appear.

continuous tone Coloured or photographic originals containing shades between the darkest and lightest tones, 'continuous' before being **screened** (broken into dots) for reproduction.

contrast The range of tonal gradations in an illustration.

control tape Computer tape containing control information rather than data.

control unit Part of a computer CPU which sequences operations.

converter A computer peripheral which transfers data from one medium to another.

copy Material for publication, especially manuscript for typesetting.

copy block A phototypesetting command treating a block of text as one unit for editing purposes.

copyfitting Determining the typographical specification to which a manuscript needs to be set in order to fill a given amount of space.

copy prep Copy preparation. Putting instructions on manuscript to ensure understanding of requirement by the compositor.

core memory Main storage capacity in the central processing unit of a computer.

corrigenda List of corrections in a book.

counter Part of a letter enclosed by strokes, such as the eye of an 'e', or space within strokes of an 'h', for example.

counting keyboard Keyboard which has logic for hyphenation and justification purposes.

CPI Characters per inch. Unit of measurement of type in a line or information on a linear storage medium.

CPP Characters per pica. Copyfitting method using average number of characters per **pica**.

CPS Characters per second. A measurement of the output speed of a phototypesetter.

CPU Central processing unit. The computing unit in an electronic system.

CRC See **camera ready copy**.

cross-head A sub-heading ranged centrally over a column.

CRPU See **camera ready paste-up**.

CRT Cathode ray tube. Images of type are exposed on a CRT in third-generation phototypesetters.

cumulative index An index which combines several other indices.

cursives Typefaces which simulate handwriting without joined characters.

cursor Moveable indicator on a screen to show a location as instructed by the operator.

cut-and-paste Traditional paste-up methods using scalpel and adhesive.

cut-in notes Notes in an outside margin of a page but which the text runs round in some degree.

cut-out Illustration with the background painted out or removed by process work.

cyrillic alphabet The Russian alphabet.

dagger Dagger-shaped symbol used as a footnote reference mark. Usually follows the asterisk in order of use.

daisy wheel Flat disk with characters on stalks used as the removable printing element of a letter-quality printer. Hence **daisy-wheel printer**.

data Information in a computer store. **Database** or **databank** is a collection of organised information from which categories may be selectively retrieved. **Data processing**, sometimes referred to as **DP**, is the generic term for the use of a computer to carry out business applications. **Data transmission** is the use of telecommunications to transfer information from one machine to another.

data communications The transmission of data between electronic devices, either in **synchronous** or **asynchronous** form.

data compression A processing technique used to save space, especially in the storage of graphics information, by eliminating redundant data and recognising communication signals on a sample basis.

dead matter Type which is finished with, or which will not be used, and may be 'killed'.

debugging The detection and correction of errors in a computer program before it goes into use.

decoding The computer process of interpreting instruction codes.

dedicated An item of equipment or electronics used for only one type of application and maybe only running one program.

dedication Inscription by the author dedicating a book to an individual. Carried among the **prelims.**

definition The degree of detail and sharpness in a reproduction.

delimiter Character used to denote the limit of a computer field.

density Measurement of the tonal value of a printed or photographic area. A **densitometer** is an instrument which measures this on an agreed scale.

depth scale Typographical ruler for measuring interlinear space.

descender The part of a character which descends below the base line, as in g, y and p.

desk top publishing Marketing term describing the concept of technically untrained office personnel producing fully page-made-up documents using a custom-made, graphics-orientated micro linked to a laser printer (a **desk top publishing system**).

diacriticals Marks attached to letters, such as the cedilla.

diamond Obsolete term for 4½pt type.

diaresis Two dots over a vowel to indicate stress.

diazo A chemical coating in photography or platemaking and the term given to a copying process which uses light-sensitive compounds (diazonium). See also **blueprint.**

Didone Group of typefaces more commonly known as **modern**, e.g. Bodoni.

didot The European measuring system for type. Based on the point of 0.376mm and named after Firmin Didot the French typefounder.

die-case Monotype matrix case.

digital computer Computer which uses binary numbers to represent and manipulate data.

digital font A typeface font converted to digital form for storage on magnetic medium.

digitisation The conversion of an image into binary form for storage and manipulation.

digitise To scan a subject and place the digitised information into computer memory for subsequent regeneration.

diphthong Letters joined together, as in æ, œ, etc.

direct access Use of a storage medium which can access information without the need for sequential searching, e.g. a disk as compared with a cassette.

direct-entry phototypesetter Self-contained phototypesetter with its own keyboard, CPU and output device.

direct impression Typewriter-style setting in which the image is created by direct impression from a type character. Also called **strike-on** composition.

dirty 1. Typesetting with many errors introduced at the keyboard. 2. Copy with many handwritten amendments.

disk 1. Computer storage device giving direct access to the information it contains. Available in various sizes and formats. 2. Circular character store used in some second generation phototypesetters.

disk drive The unit which rotates the disk in use.

discretionary hyphen Hyphen inserted by keyboard and which overrides the hyphenation program in use.

display ads Advertisements 'displayed' to occupy part or all of a page rather than set in columns.

display face A typeface designed for **display sizes** rather than for **composition sizes.**

display matter Typography set and displayed so as to be distinguished from the text, e.g. headings. Hence **display sizes** are sizes of type from 14pt upwards and **display advertisements** are those using display type.

diss Distribute. Return letterpress type to the case after printing.

distribution See **diss.**

ditto Typographic symbol for 'repeat the above matter'. Set as ″.

dot for dot Reproduction of an already screened halftone by photographing it as if it were fine line.

dot-matrix printer A computer printer which forms its printed characters from a pattern of dots.

dotless i An 'ı' available in some photocomposition fonts for the purpose of accommodating ligatures or accents.

double case A hot-metal type case combining upper and lower case.

double-density disk A **floppy disk** which can store twice as much information as its 'single-density' counterpart.

draft-quality output Low-quality high-speed wp printer output from dot-matrix printer. See also **NLQ, letter-quality output.**

dressing The loading of type fonts onto a phototypesetter.

driver Computer routine or device which handles communication between CPU and peripherals.

drop caps Drop capitals. Letters at the beginning of a paragraph which extend beyond the depth of the rest of the text line. Also called **drop initials.**

dropped heads Chapter headings positioned a few lines below the top of full text pages.

dry-transfer lettering Sheets of typographic

characters which can be transferred onto paper by rubbing.

dump Transfer a computer file into or out of storage.

duplex 1. A linecasting matrix with two characters. 2. Modems capable of sending and receiving information simultaneously.

Dvorak Keyboard layout in which the keys are positioned so as to be most readily accessible to the fingers which most often use them.

dyeline prints See **blueprints**.

E13B Magnetic ink font used on cheques.

EBCDIC Extended Binary Coded Decimal Information Code. The IBM code.

edit Check, correct and rearrange data or copy before final presentation.

editing terminal Visual display unit capable of retrieving a file and editing the contents prior to processing.

Egyptian Type style with a squared serif.

electro Electrotype. Duplicate of block or forme made by coating a mould with copper and nickel.

electronic composition Computer-assisted typesetting or page make-up.

electronic erosion Technique of creating an image by vaporising an aluminium surface coating and exposing the underlying layer of black ink.

electronic mail Transfer of documents or messages between computers or word processors using direct links, telecommunications or satellites.

electrostatic printer A device for printing an image on paper in which dark or light image areas are converted to electrostatically charged or uncharged areas on paper. Particles of fine dry powered ink adhere to the charged areas only, and are permanently fused to the paper by the application of heat. See also **xerography**.

electrotype Duplicate of block or forme made by coating a mould with metal.

elite Small size of typewriter type: 12 characters per inch.

ellipsis Three dots (. . .) indicating an omission in the copy or a pause.

em 1. Width of the body of the upper-case 'm' in any typeface. 2. Standard unit of measurement (more accurately called **pica**). One em equals 0.166044 inches.

emerald Obsolete type size of about 6½pt.

emulsion Photosensitive coating on film or plate. Hence, **emulsion side**.

en 1. Half the width of an em. Is assumed to be the width of the average type character, and so is used as the basic unit of measurement for casting off copy. 2. Fixed space of one half an em in width.

encode To code groups of characters.

end leaf See **endpaper**.

endmatter The final parts of a book after the main text: appendices, notes, index, etc.

end-of-line decisions Decisions on hyphenation or justification made either by the operator or automatically by the typesetting system.

English Obsolete type size, approximately 14pt.

enlarging/reducing system Typesetting system which creates different type sizes from a limited number of image masters.

epigraph Quotation in book prelims.

epilogue Closing section at the end of a novel or play.

EPROM Erasable Programmable Read Only Memory. Memory which can be programmed and erased by the user. Compare with **PROM**.

errata slip Slip of paper pasted into a book and containing list of author's post-press corrections.

escape code Code which signals a change of mode from, say, text to function symbols.

even pages Left-hand, or verso, pages, with even numbers.

even small caps Small capitals without full capitals.

executive program Program which organises the logistics of a computer system rather than its applications, e.g. allocates priorities of tasks.

exclusive type area Type area exclusive of headline and folio.

expanded type A typeface with characters wider in set than the standard face of the typeface family.

extended type See **expanded**.

extent Length of a book in pages.

extract Quoted matter within a text, often set indented and in a smaller type size.

fax Abbreviation for **facsimile transmission**.

face 1. The printing surface of a piece of metal type. 2. A style of type, i.e. typeface.

facing pages Pages which face each other in an open book or magazine.

facsimile 1. Exact reproduction of a document or part of it. 2. Machine which copies and transmits documents by telecommunications. Hence **facsimile transmission (fax)**.

fair copy A correction-free copy of a document.

family A collection of all fonts and sizes based on one basic typeface design.

feed holes Holes in paper tape used by the sprocket on the mechanical reader to feed the tape in.

feet The base of a piece of metal type.

fibre-optic cable A protective glass or plastic cable containing a pure fibre of the same material, used to transmit light from **LEDs** or **lasers** in the communication of signals.

fibre optics The technique of communicating data by the transmission of light through plastic or glass fibres.

field A predefined area of a computer record.

file A collection of related computer records.

filler advertisement Advertisement used to occupy redundant space rather than booked for insertion.

film advance The distance by which film in a photosetter advances between lines of type to create interlinear space or 'leading'. Also called **film feed** or **line feed**.

film feed See **film advance**.

film make-up Positioning pieces of film ready for platemaking. **Page make-up** is used as the term for pages or **assembly** for full imposition.

film mechanical Camera-ready material composed in film rather than paper.

filmsetting Loose term for phototypesetting.

FIPP International Federation of the Periodical Press.

firmware Software which is necessary for the

general routines of a computer and which cannot be changed by the user. Usually held in **ROM.**

first generation Early photosetters modelled after hot-metal machines and largely mechanical in operation.

first proof The earliest proof used for checking by proof readers.

first revise The corrected proof made after errors noted on the first proof have been re-set.

fit The relative closeness of typeset characters to each other; fit can be expanded or reduced by most modern typesetting systems.

fixed-head A disk drive in which the read-write heads do not move.

fixed space An amount of space between letters and words which is not varied for justification needs.

flag An indicator in a program which marks the position of data or signals a condition to the program. In a typeset file a mark which denotes an item for a specific application e.g. index extraction, colour splitting.

flat artwork Artwork which is drawn on a solid base and which cannot therefore be directly scanned on a drum scanner.

flatbed scanner A scanner with a flat platen, rather like a photocopier, as opposed to one with a scanning drum.

flat plan Diagrammatic scheme of the pagination of a magazine.

fleuron A typographical flower ornament used for decorative purposes.

floating accents Accents which are not tied to a given character in a type font and can therefore be positioned over any letter.

floppy disk Small flexible plastic disk widely used for magnetic storage of information on microcomputers.

flush left/right Type aligned with either the left- or right-hand margins.

FOC Father of Chapel. Print union equivalent of shop steward.

foliation The numbering of manuscript pages.

folio Page number at the head or foot of text.

font A complete set of characters all of the same typeface design and point size. Also known as **fount,** especially in hot metal.

foot Bottom of a book or page.

footnotes Notes explanatory to the main text, set in smaller type at the bottom of the page.

foreword Introduction to a book, not written by the author.

format 1. The physical specification for a page or a book. 2. Frequently occurring set of typographical commands stored as a code on a phototypesetter.

forme Metal type and other matter locked up in a chase ready for printing.

foundry chase Chase used in stereo making.

foundry lockup A forme locked up for making moulds of electrotypes, stereotypes etc.

foundry type Hard-wearing metal type characters used in hand composition.

fount See **font.**

fourth generation Output device using lasers for exposure of the image.

front end General term for the parts of a typesetting system used to prepare data for the output device, e.g. keyboards, editing terminals, computers, etc.

full out Set flush with no indentations.

full point Full stop.

function codes Codes which control the function of a phototypesetter rather than generating characters.

furniture Letterpress spacing material.

galley 1. Shallow tray used to hold a column of metal type. 2. Proof pulled from a galley of type. 3. Film or bromide output in unpaged form.

galley stepover Reversal of film or paper transport in a typesetting machine to allow galleys of text to be set side-by-side, as for multi-column work.

Garalde Generic term for the group of typefaces also known as **Old Face.**

generic coding Methods of mark-up, such as **ASPIC** or **SGML,** defining a document typographically or structurally. The codes are programmed to convert into typesetting functions.

gigabyte See **byte.** The prefix giga- denotes one thousand million (10^9).

global search and replace The facility of a computer program to find all examples of a word or group of words in a file and replace them with an alternative.

glossary Alphabetically arranged list of terms and their meanings.

glyphic Typeface based on a chiselled rather than a calligraphic form.

golfball A removable typeface carrier shaped like a golfball such as is found on early IBM **strike-on** composition equipment.

gothic Typeface or script of black letter design.

graphic Typeface whose design suggests it has been drawn rather than written.

graphic display terminal VDU capable of displaying pictures in line or tone.

graphics Pictures and illustrations either in line or tone in printed work.

graphics tablet Calibrated tablet on which, using a **light-pen** or **mouse,** an operator brings together components of a design and fixes them electronically in their correct positions according to the required layout.

gray scale Strip of grey tones from white to black, used to measure tonal range against a standard.

great primer Obsolete term for 18pt type.

grid Sheet with ruled lines used to ensure square make-up of photocomposed or displayed material.

h&j Hyphenation and justification.

hairline Very fine line or stroke in a letter.

hair spaces In metal composition, a very thin space $\frac{1}{5}$ of an em of set or less. Often used for letterspacing characters in a word and still employed in phototypesetting to describe a very fine space of indeterminate width.

half title Title of book, sometimes shortened, printed on right-hand page before title page. Sometimes called **bastard title.**

halftone Process by which continuous tone is simulated by a pattern or screen of dots of varying size.

hand setting The composition of lines of metal type by hand, usually in a 'stick'.

hanging indent Typesetting style in which the first line of a paragraph is set full out and the remainder are indented.

hard copy Copy written, typed or printed as distinct from stored in electronic form.

hard hyphen Hyphen grammatically essential to a word. See **soft hyphen.**

hardware Computer term for equipment as distinct from programs.

hard-wired Circuit or program as constructed by the manufacturer of a piece of hardware and which cannot be changed.

head Top – or top margin – of a page.

headline A displayed line or lines at the top of a page or a piece of text. See also **running head.**

headliner Phototypesetting machine designed to produce lines of display-sized type.

head margin The white space between the top edge of the page and the first line of type.

heading See **headline.**

height to paper Standard height of metal type and blocks. Varies from country to country.

highlights Lightest tonal values in a halftone.

holding lines Design lines which indicate the area of a piece of artwork on a page.

host 1. Main central processing unit in a multi-computer system. 2. Holder of an on-line database.

hot metal Type cast in metal by linecasting or single-letter composition machines.

house advertisement **Filler advertisement** for a periodical's own company.

house copies Copies of a magazine for use within the publishing house rather than for sale.

house corrections Proofs altered by the publisher or printer, as distinct from author's corrections.

house style See **style of the house.**

Humanist Generic term for 'Venetian' style typefaces.

hybrid Twentieth-century typeface designs adapted for phototypesetting from a combination of earlier designs.

hyphenation exception dictionary A collection of words which cannot be broken grammatically by normal rules of **hyphenation logic** and is stored in memory with fixed hyphenation points for access during the **h&j** process.

hyphenation logic Program by which words are broken at line ends according to rules of derivation, constructed from syllable, prefix, suffix and root-word analysis. See also **hyphenation exception dictionary.**

hyphenless justification Justification without breaking words. In general, this creates more widely varying spacing characteristics than hyphenation and justification.

icon A graphic symbol used in screen displays to represent a function, e.g. wastepaper basket, filing cabinet, folder.

idiot copy Unformatted copy with no line ending commands.

image master Photographic original for photosetting fonts. Also, **film master.**

imagesetter An output recorder which can set type and graphics. This normally requires a laser imaging system.

impact printer Printer where the printing element strikes the paper through a ribbon, e.g. daisy wheel or golfball.

imprint Publisher's and/or printer's identifying text printed in a book or other work.

inclusive type area Type area inclusive of headline and folio.

indent Type set further in from the left-hand margin than the standard measure of surrounding text.

index Alphabetical list of subjects contained in the text of a work, together with their page references.

indexing The jagged edges occasionally visible in digitised type, resulting from insufficient resolution in the output device.

inferior Small character set below the base line at the foot of another character.

information retrieval The accessing by computer of text held in an electronic file.

initial First letter in text set in such a way that it stands out, e.g. bigger than its normal cap text size.

initialise Run a program which sets up a storage medium such as a floppy disk to be compatible with the system in use.

ink-jet printer A **non-impact printing** (qv) mechanism which forms the image at high speed by deflecting ink droplets electromagnetically.

input keyboard Keyboard used primarily to enter text into a typesetting system.

instruction Order in a program telling a computer to carry out an operation.

integrated book Book with text and pictures together throughout (as opposed to pictures in a plate section).

interactive Computer system used in real time so that the operator can issue commands which affect the processing.

interactive terminal Workstation at which changes are effected and displayed as they are made.

interface The link between parts of a computer system, varying from a simple cable to an 'intelligent' device which translates protocol.

interlinear space Space between lines in photocomposition of text. See **film advance, film feed.**

intermediates Films used in the intermediate stages of reproduction between the original and final printing films.

Intertype Proprietary name of a linecasting machine similar to a **Linotype.**

I/O Input/Output Relating to systems which can input and output to and from a computer.

ion deposition Printing process based on the adherence of a conductive toner to an electrically charged image area.

italic Originally cursive handwriting as found in Italian manuscripts of the 14th and 15th centuries, now understood to mean almost any inclined character; often used in text matter for emphasis. Distinguished from electronically slanted roman type by differences of serif structure and cursive 'feel'.

jobbing General printing.

justification The adjustment of spacing between words to give 'straight' left and right margins.

K kilobyte; a measure of computer storage. 1Kb=1024 bytes (or Kb) (often used loosely as 1000).

keep standing Instruction to keep metal type made up for possible reprinting.

kern That part of a character which overhangs a neighbouring character.

kerning In phototypesetting, the reduction, by computer controlled operation, of space between characters.

keyboard The array of keys used to input into a system.

keystroke One key depression, often used as a measure of productivity of an operator.

kicker Short line above a headline, set in smaller type.

kill Delete unwanted matter.

LAN Local Area Network. A network of interfaced peripherals linked by cable over a limited area (e.g. an office environment), allowing two-way communication between users.

language In computing and communications, a set of characters, representations and rules for communicating information, e.g. ALGOL, FORTRAN, BASIC.

laser Acronym for Light Amplification By Stimulated Emission of Radiation. Concentrated light beam used to create images, engraving, etc.

laser printer A printer in which digitised characters and images are exposed by laser beam onto a charged drum, and transferred to plain paper by **xerography** (qv).

latent image The latent electrostatic image generated by a photocopier and which powder turns into a visible image.

lateral reversal Change of image from left- to right-reading or vice versa.

Latin alphabet Western European alphabet.

layout Plan of page or area to be composed, showing relative position of all type and graphic elements.

layout terminal See **page make-up terminal.**

leader Row of dots used to lead the eye across a page.

lead-in The introduction in a piece of setting, often in a bold or different face.

leading The spacing between lines of type (strips of lead in metal composition).

LEDs Light Emitting Diodes. Semiconducting light sources used in imaging systems as an alternative to laser technology.

legend Caption.

legibility The ease with which the individual characters of a particular typeface can be identified. See **readability.**

Letraset Proprietary name of sheets of transfer lettering.

letterfit The degree to which characters in any typeface appear closely or loosely fitted together.

letterpress Printing from images with a raised surface which impress on the paper.

letter-quality output Slow-speed, good quality wp printer output, typical of daisy-wheel printers.

letter space Space inserted between characters.

ligature Two or more letters joined together on one body (ff, fi, fl, ffi, ffl).

light gate array An array of cells which can be programmed to allow or prevent light passing through to expose photographic material in the creation of an image.

lineale Typeface without serifs, otherwise known as **sans-serif.**

linecaster Machine which casts complete lines of metal type, e.g. a Linotype.

line feed See **film advance.**

line gauge Measuring ruler used for copy-fitting and measuring type. Also called **type gauge** and **depth gauge** or **depth scale.**

line printer Output device which prints one line at a time usually with non-letter-quality resolution.

linespacing Space between lines of photoset type.

lining figures Arabic numerals the same height as capitals. As distinct from **non-lining** or **old-style figures.**

Linotype 1. Manufacturer of digital typesetting equipment. 2. Linecasting machine formerly manufactured by Linotype, now L&M, a separate company.

listing Computer print-out of data or a file.

literal Mistake introduced in keyboarding, often affecting only one or two characters.

lith film A high contrast film.

lithography Planographic process in which ink is applied selectively to the plate by chemically treating image areas to accept ink and non-image areas to accept water. Shortened to **litho.**

litho prep American terminology for repro, film make-up and other pre-press camerawork.

lock up To secure metal type in a forme ready for the next stage of production.

logo scanner A device which converts a logo, or other special symbol, into digital signals for computer input and display on a VDU. The image may then be manipulated or changed in some way before output.

logotype 1. Company name or product device used in a special design as a trademark. Shortened to **logo.** 2. In metal composition, a whole name or word cast and used as one piece of type.

long primer Obsolete type size, approximately 10pt.

lower case Small letters as distinct from capitals. Abbreviated as **lc.** See **upper case.**

Ludlow Proprietary name of a display-size type-casting machine which uses hand-assembled matrices.

machine code Primary code used by the computer's processor.

machine composition General term for composition of metal type using typecasting equipment.

macro Single keystroke programmed to activate the commands necessary to access special characters, symbols, etc.

magazine The container for storing matrices on linecasting machines.

magnetic inks Inks with magnetic content that can be read by electronic sensing. Used on cheques.

magnetic tape Narrow tape magnetically coated for the storage in serial form of computer data.

magnetography Printing process based on the magnetisation of tiny recording heads by digital data, creating an image area to which magnetic toner adheres.

mainframe Large computer.

make-up Making up typeset material into pages.

manuscript Abbreviated to **MS.** Typed or handwritten copy for setting.

marching display Visual display of one line of

type displayed sequentially as keyboarded.

margins Areas of white space left around printed matter on a page.

mark up Instructions on a layout or copy for the compositor to follow when typesetting or making up pages.

marked proof The proof on which the printer's reader has marked corrections.

master proof Printer's proof or reader's proof. See also **marked proof.**

masthead Graphic device which displays a newspaper's name on the front page.

mat See **matrix.**

match (or merge) and drop Process of eliminating repetition of the same term in computerised data sorting. See **match (or merge) and replace.**

match (or merge) and replace Process of merging, by computer, duplicate appearances of the same term in data sorting, or replacing it with predefined characters. See **match (or merge) and drop.**

matrix 1. In metal typecasting, the recessed die which imparts the design of the letter onto the face of the type being cast. 2. The photographic image master of a character.

Mb Abbreviation for **megabyte** (qv).

mean-line Imaginary line level with the tops of lower case letters. Also called **x-line.**

measure Length of a line of type.

mechanical Camera-ready paste-up.

mechanical composition See **machine composition.**

media converter Hardware device which converts computer coded data into intelligible information.

megabyte Unit of computer storage; 1Mb=1,000Kb, or 1 million bytes.

memory Internal storage of a computer.

menu The display of a list of functions available for selection by an operator.

menu-driven Software program laid out in the initial form of a number of questions to which the operator replies in order to action the program.

merge Combine two or more files into one.

metric system The decimal system of measurement.

microcomputer Small computer, usually without multi-user capabilities.

microfiche Sheet film, in size typically 105×150mm, containing on it a large number of pages of information photographically reduced to very small size and readable only with a **microfiche reader.**

microform Generic term for **microfiche.**

microprocessor See **microcomputer.**

microsecond One-millionth part of a second. Measurement used in computing.

middle space or **mid space** Fixed space equal to one-quarter of a 'mutton' or em space.

middle tones Tonal range between highlights and shadows.

'milking machine' Colloquial term for portable text retrieval device which records data on to a cassette tape or disk, to be downloaded to a typesetting system through its RS232C port.

millisecond One-thousandth part of a second. Measurement used in computing.

minicomputer Powerful computer, between mainframe and micro in size, usually dedicated to one job rather than general data processing.

minion Obsolete term for 7pt type.

mixing Usually applied to typefaces of different fonts in one line of text.

mock-up A layout or rough of artwork. Also called **visual.**

modem or **Mo**dulator/**Dem**odulator. Device which converts analog communication (e.g. telephone transmission) into digital form and vice versa.

Modern Late 18th-century type style, also called **Didone.**

modern figures See **lining figures.**

modular Hardware system capable of being expanded by adding on compatible devices.

mono See **black and white.**

monoline Typeface with all strokes appearing to have the same thickness, e.g. Univers.

Monophoto Proprietary name of a British photosetting system.

monospaced Typesetting system in which all characters have identical set widths.

Monotype Proprietary name of a 'hot-metal' typecasting machine which assembles characters individually rather than line by line.

mould In metal typecasting, the shape through which hot metal is forced, creating the rectangular metal body on which the character is cast.

mouse A palm-sized unit with buttons, attached to the display terminal, and used in preference to the keyboard to manipulate the screen display. The mouse is moved by the operator over a tablet, and its movement is monitored by the computer. Different control functions are accessed by the use of buttons on the mouse, or by moving the mouse to defined 'menu' areas on the tablet. Used to position elements of a job in electronic page make-up systems.

MS See **manuscript.**

multi-disk reader Device capable of reading many kinds of disks, varying in size, storage capacity and recording density. The information can be written onto new disks, with the existing codings converted as relevant.

multiplexor Device enabling communication between central storage and peripherals.

multiprocessing Concurrent computer processing of several tasks.

multitasking See **multiprocessing.**

mutton An em quad.

nanosecond One-thousand-millionth part of a second. Measurement of computer processing speed.

narrow band Data transmission at speeds lower than 200 bits per second.

negative Photographic image on film in which dark and light areas appear exactly transposed from the original.

newspaper lines per minute Standard measure of photosetter speeds. Specifically, output measured in 8pt lines to an 11em measure.

NGA National Graphical Association, the UK print union.

nick Groove in metal type which appears uppermost during assembly.

NLQ Near Letter Quality. Used to describe higher-density dot-matrix printer output. Between **draft quality** and **letter quality** output.

noise Disturbance on an electrical circuit.

non-counting keyboards Keyboards which cannot access justification logic and whose output therefore must be h&j'd either by the front-end system or the typesetting machine itself.

non-impact printing Electronic methods of image transfer without striking paper. See **ink-jet printer, laser printer.**

non-lining figures Also called **old-style figures.** Numerals which do not align on the base line but have ascenders and descenders. As distinct from **modern** or **lining figures.**

nonpareil Obsolete term for 6pt type.

nut An en quad.

object program Machine intelligible program.

OCR The interpretation of typewritten characters by a machine which scans the text and stores it in memory, often for subsequent typesetting.

OCR paper High-quality bond suitable for optical character recognition equipment.

OEM Original Equipment Manufacturer. Acronym (and misnomer) for manufacturer who buys original equipment, adds features (and therefore value) before re-selling as a new package.

off-line Mode of computer peripheral operation in which equipment is not physically linked to a CPU and must be operated through an intermediate medium, by disk or tape.

offset Printing which uses an intermediate medium to transfer the image on to paper, e.g. a rubber blanket wrapped around a cylinder as in offset litho.

Old Face Early 17th-century type style. Also called **Garalde.**

old-style figures See **non-lining figures.**

on-demand publishing The concept of printing books one at a time from computer store 'on demand', rather than tying up capital by printing for stock.

on-line Mode of computer peripheral operation in which equipment is connected direct to, and communicating with, a central processing unit.

'on the fly' Colloquialism for process which occurs as output is being performed, such as the screening of halftones as they are output to an imagesetter.

opacity The quality of opaqueness in a paper.

operation Result of a computer command.

optical centre The 'visual' centre of a page, about 10% higher than the mathematical centre.

optical character recognition See **OCR.**

optical digital disk A **video disk** which stores information as bits of data, rather than as visual images, allowing large amounts of data to be written on to a small surface. See **optical disk, CD-ROM.**

optical disk A disk which holds data in a series of indentations etched onto its surface, and read by laser beam. See **optical digital disk, video disk, CD-ROM.**

optical letterspacing Space between letters which accommodates their varying shapes and gives the appearance of even space.

original Photograph or drawing to be reproduced.

origination All the processes involved in the reproduction of original material, including make-up, up to platemaking stages, and also including typesetting.

ornamented Typeface embellished with decorative flourishes.

orphan First line of a paragraph at foot of page. Considered undesirable.

orthochromatic Photographic materials sensitive to yellow, blue and green rays but not red.

outline Typeface comprising only an outline with no 'solid' area.

output Data or any form of communication coming out of a computer after processing.

output recorder Loose description of any machine capable of outputting type and graphics by non-photographic means, and therefore distinguishable from a **phototypesetter.** See **imagesetter.**

overmatter Typeset matter which was not used in the final printing.

ozalid Form of copying process often used for proofing film. See also **blueprint.**

package Set of software bought 'off the shelf' rather than specifically written for a purpose.

packing density Amount of information which can be stored on a magnetic medium.

page description language Software necessary for the composition of combined text and graphics, encompassing factors such as scaling, font rotation, graphics and angles. Some examples, such as Adobe's Postscript, are device-independent. Other contenders in the market are Interpress from Xerox, DDL from Imagen Corporation and Interleaf's RIPprint.

page make-up Assembly of the elements in a page into their final design.

page-make-up terminal Specialised workstation used to electronically assemble type and graphics into finished page form.

page proof Proof of a page before printing.

page-view terminal VDU which can display a page in its made-up form.

pagination 1. The batch processing of volume data into a sequence of composed pages. Compare with **page make-up.** 2. The numbering of a set of pages in sequence.

paper tape Strip of paper which records data as a series of punched holes arranged in 'channels' or 'tracks' across the width.

paragraph opener Typographic device marking the start of a paragraph which needs emphasising, e.g. □.

parameter A variable set to a constant value for a specific operation.

parenthesis Pair of marks, ( ), used for interpolation in text.

parity bit A check bit added to a series of binary digits to make the total odd or even according to the logic of the system.

paste-up Dummy or artwork comprising all the elements pasted into position.

patch Corrections pasted or stripped over or into original setting.

patching Pasting corrections into film or artwork.

pc personal computer Microcomputer for home or office use.

PE printer's error Normally a literal in typesetting.

peculiars Special characters outside a normal font range.

perforated tape See **paper tape.**

perforating Punching a series of holes in paper, as a coding process.

perforator Keyboard which produces punched paper tape.

peripheral Computer input or output device which is not part of the main CPU, e.g. a printer.

photocomposition Typesetting performed by a phototypesetter.

photocopy 1. Duplicate of a photograph. 2. Duplicate of a document, etc., produced on a copying machine.

photogravure Printing process in which the image is held in a screen of tiny cells on the surface of a cylinder. These cells are filled with ink which is transferred by contact to the paper. Used for long-run magazines and catalogues.

photolettering Method of setting display-sized type from photographic fonts.

photolithography Lithographic process with photographically produced plate image.

photomechanical transfer Abbreviated to **PMT.** Paper negative which produces a positive print by a process of chemical transfer.

photosetting See **phototypesetting.**

phototypesetting Typesetting using photographic principles, i.e. film masters, lens systems and light sources. Hence **phototypesetter.** See **imagesetter, output recorder.**

pi characters Special characters outside the normal alphabetic range and not normally contained in a standard font, e.g. special maths symbols. Some typesetting manufactuers now hold a huge variety of special symbols.

pica 1. Unit of typographic measurement equal to 12 points or 4.21mm. 2. Size of typewriter face with 10 characters to the inch.

pie Jumbled metal type. Sometimes spelt **pi.**

pitch Measurement of the number of characters per horizontal inch in typewriter faces.

pixel The minute individual image/non-image areas created by the digitisation of type or graphics. A pixel is the smallest element of a digital image that can be addressed.

planning All the processes involved in imposition, laying pages down onto foils in imposition sequence, etc., ready for platemaking.

PMT See **photomechanical transfer.**

point size Description of a size of type. Not usually directly equivalent to the size of the printed image of this type.

point system The main system of typographic measurement. 1pt=.013837″ or 0.351mm. See also **didot, em, pica.**

port An input and/or output connection to or from a computer.

portrait The shape of an image or page with the shorter dimensions at the head and foot.

positive An image on film or paper in which the dark and light values are the same as the original, as distinct from **negative.**

PPA Periodical Publishers Association.

preface Formal statement before the text of a book by the author. As distinct from **foreword.**

prelims Abbreviation of **preliminary matter.** The matter in a book which precedes the text.

pre-press costs All the costs associated with bringing a job ready for press up to but not including printing the first copy. As distinct from **press costs.**

pre-screened illustration Illustration original which is already screened in halftone form. Subsequent reproduction handles such an originals 'dot for dot', with each existing screen dot recognized by the camera as a line image.

press costs The costs associated with printing and manufacturing a job from plates onwards. As distinct from **pre-press costs.**

preview screen. A VDU which allows a piece of composed work to be viewed exactly as it will appear in print. See **soft typesetter.**

printer's error See **PE.**

print-out The text printed out by a computer printer.

program The complete set of instructions which control a computer in the performance of a task.

PROM Programmable Read Only Memory. Memory which can be programmed but not subsequently altered by the user. See **ROM, EPROM.**

proof A trial printed sheet or copy, made before the production run, for the purpose of checking.

proofreader's marks Symbols used by a proofreader in marking corrections on proofs.

proofreading Checking typeset proofs.

protocol Set of conventions controlling the exchange of data between communicating devices.

pseudo font Typeface used to represent text with character widths (and therefore line endings) from a different typeface. This allows text to be proofed via laser printers in typefaces for which the relevant low-resolution font information is not available.

puck See **mouse.**

pull 1. A proof (metal composition). 2. A single print for subsequent photo-litho reproduction, often called a **repro pull.**

punch In hot-metal typefounding, the relief image of a character used to create a matrix.

punched tape See **paper tape.**

quad Letterpress spacing material used to fill out lines of type.

quad left, right or centre To set lines flush left, right or centre.

quoin An expanding wedge used to lock up letterpress chases.

quotes Inverted commas.

QWERTY Standard typewriter-keyboard layout, QWERTY being the arrangement of keys on the top left-hand row of the board.

RAGA Reproduction and Graphics Association.

ragged right Text with an even left margin but an uneven right margin.

random access Method of directly accessing a specific address on a computer file without the need for a sequential process. **Random access memory** is often abbreviated to **RAM.**

range Align (type, etc.).

rapid-access processing Method of quick film and paper processing using heated chemicals.

raster image processor (RIP) Device which organises the symbolic description of a page made up of individual **pixels** and pre-defines this description into the scan lines needed for output to a laser device. See **bitmap.**

raster scan The technique of recording an image line by line in sweeps across the whole image area.

raw data Data before processing or preparation.

readability The ease with which printed matter composed in a given typeface can be assimilated. See **legibility**.

reader 1. Person who checks proofs for accuracy. 2. Device which can 'read' from magnetic media or in the case of OCR, from typescript.

reader's proof First proof used by the printer's reader.

reading head See **read/write head**.

read/write head The component which reads from and writes to a magnetic disk or tape.

real time Method of computing in which operations are performed on data simultaneously with input and output.

recall To call a computer file from backing store into memory.

record A block of computer data.

recto A right-hand page.

reflection copy Copy viewed by its reflected light, e.g. a photograph, as distinct from **transmission copy**.

reformatting Setting new typographical parameters for a previously set piece of copy.

refresh rate Rate at which an image is flashed on a VDU, e.g. 60 times a second, etc.

repro Pre-press camerawork, scanning and film make-up.

repro paper Coated paper suitable for use in camera-ready artwork. Also called **baryta paper**.

repro pull See **reproduction proof**.

reproduction proof A proof taken from metal type for subsequent reproduction.

resin-coated paper Abbreviated to **RC paper**. Photographic paper with good longevity of image used in phototypesetting.

resolution The definition or sharpness of characters produced by digital imagesetters, usually measured in terms of 'lpi', the number of output strokes per inch used to create the image. The resolution of an imagesetter usually varies in inverse proportion to output speed.

response time The time taken to display the result of a command on a VDU.

retouching Correcting a photographic print or transparency before reproduction.

reverse leading Ability of a phototypesetter to move film or paper 'backwards', used in column or tabular work.

reverse out Type printing white out of another colour.

reverse reading See **wrong reading**.

revise A revised proof for subsequent reading.

right reading Film which reads 'correctly', i.e. from left to right, as distinct from **wrong reading**.

rigid disk Aluminium-based disk with magnetic coating, of greater storage capacity and less corruptible than a **floppy disk**. Needs a carefully controlled environment to avoid corruption.

RIP See **raster image processor**.

river Undesirable formation of word spaces into a vertical 'river' of white in the text.

ROM or **Read Only Memory** Computer memory which cannot be altered by the user.

roman figures Roman numerals such as iii, xviii, xxv, etc.

roman type 1. 'Upright' letters as distinct from **italic**. 2. Type of normal weight as distinct from bold or light. Usually clear from context which sense is.

rough proof Proof for identification rather than reading.

routine A computer program with a selective task.

ruby See **agate**.

rule A line (of specified thickness).

run The activation of a computer program.

run-around Type set around a picture or other element of design.

run on Continue copy on same line.

running head A title repeated at the top of each page. Also known as **running headline**.

same-size system Typesetting system which holds unique image master for each type size.

sans serif A typeface with no **serifs**.

scaling Calculating the enlargement or reduction of an original for reproduction.

scanner Electronic device which reads the relative densities of an image and records the information, usually in digital form.

screen The dot formation in **halftones**.

screen ruling The number of lines or dots per inch on a screen.

screened negative See **halftone**.

screened positive See **halftone**.

script A typeface which simulates handwriting.

scrolling Moving text vertically or horizontally into and out of the display area of a VDU.

second generation Photosetters using electro-mechanical means of exposing type.

sequential access Reading items in computer memory in sequence rather than by **random access** (qv).

series A set of fonts of the same design, but graded in size.

serif Short terminal stroke at end of main stroke of a typographic character.

set 1. To typeset. 2. The width of a character.

SETM Specifying Electronic Typographic Markup. New language for typographic mark-up of text, proposed by BSI in April 1987.

set width See **set**.

SGML Standard Generalized Mark-up Language. A system of text coding for electronic manuscripts, devised in the USA and now a Draft International Standard. It defines a document by its structure. See **generic coding**.

shank In hot-metal, the stem of a piece of type.

shift A key which, when depressed, gives a different designation to all the other keys, e.g. turns a lower-case letter into upper case.

shoulder notes See **side notes**.

shoulder head A heading in text, ranged left in a line on its own.

show-through Lack of opacity in a sheet of paper to the point where the printed image on one side of a page is excessively visible from the reverse side.

side-head Heading ranged left with the text.

side-notes Short lines of text set in the margins.

single tasking Computer system capable of performing only one operation at a time.

slab serif Typeface with heavy, square-ended serifs. Also known as **Egyptian**.

slave or **slave unit** A remote device which is driven by logic from a central processing unit.

sloped roman A synthetic (as distinct from 'true') italic form created by third-generation typesetting machines and their successors by electronic slanting of the roman form.

slug Line of metal type cast in one piece.

small caps An alphabet of capitals designed to the same size as the x-height of the normal lower case.

small pica Obsolete term for 11pt type.

soft copy Non-paper version of text, e.g. on a VDU.

soft hyphen Hyphen introduced in a word by the h&j program. See **hard hyphen**.

soft typesetter A VDU, such as a **preview screen**, usually non-interactive, showing an exact replica of a piece of work as it will appear in print. See **WYSIWYG**.

software Computer programs.

SOGAT Society of Graphical and Allied Trades, one of the UK unions for trades closely associated with printing.

solid Type set with no extra interlinear space.

sort 1. A single character of metal type. 2. To order data into a given sequence, e.g. alphabetical.

spacebands Spacing wedges used by linecasting machines.

spaces Pieces of metal type used to space out letters or words.

spec Specification.

special sort Unusual character necessary in a job.

specimen Sample setting used as a check on the typographic specification.

spelling-check program A computer program which checks the accuracy of each word of input against the spellings of a dictionary held in memory.

spiking Inconstant surges in power on an electrical power line causing interference with sensitive electronic equipment.

spot colour Single additional colour used in the printing of a job.

spread Pair of facing pages.

sprocket holes Feed holes in paper tape.

s/s Abbreviation for 'same size' in reproduction specifications.

stabilisation paper Photographic paper used for phototypesetting output. Has short image-retention span once processed and will discolour.

stand-alone A self-contained hardware system which needs no other machine assistance to function.

standing type Metal type stored after printing or proofing pending subsequent re-use.

stem Main stroke of a letter or figure.

stereotype Duplicate printing plate cast in a mould taken from the original. Abbreviated to **stereo**.

stet Proofreader's instruction meaning 'ignore marked correction', i.e. let it stand as it was.

stick See **composing stick**.

stone The surface (now metal) on which pages of metal type are assembled and planed down (levelled).

storage Computer memory or a magnetic medium which can store information, e.g. a floppy disk.

straight matter Straightforward text setting.

stress Angle of shading in typeface character design. May be oblique or vertical.

strike-on composition Typesetting created by direct impression of image-carrying surface, e.g. typewriter composition.

string A sequence of alphabetic or numeric characters in a computer program.

stripper film Very thin film used for hand corrections.

stripping Film handling, correction and assembly (American).

stump Term coined by the typesetting systems manufacturer Miles 33 to describe a hyphenated word at foot of column or page. Considered undesirable.

style of the house Typographic and linguistic rules of a publishing house. Also **house style**.

sub 1. Sub editor: journalist who edits copy. 2. Subscription to a magazine or journal.

subscript Inferior character. Small character printed below the base line as part of mathematical equation.

superior Small character set above the line, especially used in mathematical statements (e.g. 10^2) or to indicate footnotes; also called **superscript**.

swash letter An ornamental italic character, usually a cap.

swelled rules Rules which are wider at the centre than at the ends.

synchronous transmission Method of data transmission in which streams of data are transmitted at a given rate between a perfectly synchronised transmitter and receiver.

systems functions Functions relating to the movement of data within a system and controlled from the keyboard, e.g. writing to memory, or transmission between peripherals.

tabular material Typeset tables or columns of figures.

tail Downward stroke of a letter.

take An amount of copy for typesetting allocated to one operator.

tape merging The combination of data from a master tape and a correction tape to produce a third, error-free tape.

tape transport The device which moves tape past the reading heads.

telecommunications Communication over the telephone wire.

teletypesetter Abbreviated to **TTS**. Linecasting system driven by six-channel paper tape generated on separate keyboards.

terminal Keyboard and/or screen for computer communication or text generation.

text The body typesetting in a book as distinct from headings and display type.

text pages The principal matter in a book as distinct from the prelims, index, etc.

text type Body type of a printed work. Loosely, type smaller than about 12pt.

thick space Fixed space equal to one-third of an em.

thin space Fixed space equal to one-fifth of an em.

third generation Typesetting machines using cathode ray tubes to generate images.

time-sharing Concurrent processing of several jobs or programs on a computer.

title page Page of a book carrying the title,

author's name and publisher's name. Always recto.

torn-tape system Paper-tape typesetting system involving manual removal and feeding of tape from one machine to another.

track A path on which information is carried on a sequential storage medium such as tape or disk.

transfer type Pressure-sensitive type on carrier sheets. Can be 'rubbed-off' to create type in position. Also known as **transfer lettering.**

Transitional Type style such as Baskerville which evolved between **Old Style** and **Modern.**

transmission copy Copy which is viewed by transmitted light, e.g. a transparency.

transpose Abbreviated **trs.** Exchange the position of words, letters or lines, especially on a proof. Hence **transposition.**

TS Abbreviation for typescript.

TTS See **teletypesetter.**

'turnkey' systems Systems based on standard hardware, developed for specific applications.

type area Area occupied by text on a page.

typecasting Casting type in metal by a machine such as a Linotype or Monotype.

typeface A specifically designated style of type, e.g. Times or Helvetica.

type gauge A rule calibrated in picas for measuring type.

type metal The alloy for cast type, comprising lead, tin and antimony.

type scale See **type gauge.**

typewriter composition See **strike-on composition.**

typographer Designer of printed material.

typographic errors Abbreviated to **typos.** See **literals.**

u and lc also **u/lc** Abbreviation for upper and lower case. Instruction to follow copy for caps and lower case.

UDF An instruction assigned to an input key to access a particular command or string of commands over and above any normal function; keys programmable by the user in this way are also known as UDKs (User Defined Keys), user programmable keys, or macros.

unit Division of the em measurement into smaller units of width used to allocate different widths to different characters.

unit value The number of units in a character. See **unit.**

unjustified Text set with an even right or left edge with even spacing and therefore a ragged left or right edge. Setting ranged left (unjustified) is also known as **ragged right,** setting ranged right (unjustified) as **ragged left.**

un-shift Keyboard designation for lower case.

update Edit a file by adding current data.

upper case Capital letters. See **lower case.**

variable space Space between words used to justify a line.

VDU/VDT See **visual display unit/terminal.**

vector scanning A method of storing a digital typographic image by vectors or outlines.

verso Left-hand page with even number.

vertical justification Spacing a column of

type to fit a set depth. Automatic process on some typesetting systems.

video disk An optical disk which stores information as visual images rather than digital data. See **optical disk, optical digital disk, CD-ROM.**

visual A layout or rough of artwork.

visual display unit/terminal Cathode-ray tube screen and keyboard for input and editing of copy.

weight In typography, the degree of boldness of a typeface style (e.g. light, medium, etc).

wf Wrong font. Proofreader's mark indicating a character from an incorrect font has been used in setting.

white line Line of space in phototypesetting.

widow Short last line of a paragraph at the top of a page. Considered undesirable.

WIMPS Acronym for the set of features—Windows, Icons, Mouse and Puck—often provided as aids for the manipulation of data by a workstation operator. See **icon, mouse, puck, windows.**

Winchester disk Hard disk with extensive backing store capacity.

Winchester disk drive Sealed unit of multiple rigid disks.

window 1. Clear panel left in litho film for halftones to be stripped in. 2. A description of the contents of different computer files on screen for easy viewing by the operator.

word break Division of a word at a line ending.

word processor Machine using computer logic to accept, store and retrieve documents for subsequent editing and output.

word space The variable space between words which may be increased or decreased to justify a line.

WORM Acronym for Write Once Read Many, an optical digital disk on which data can be recorded but not erased by the user.

workstation Part of a computer typesetting system manned by an operator, e.g. an editing terminal.

wp See **word processor.**

write To record or output electronic data.

wrong font See **wf.**

wrong-reading Film which reads 'incorrectly', i.e. reversed from left to right.

WYSIWYG What You See Is What You Get. Acronym used to describe a visual display showing an exact replica of typeface, size and relative position of all elements of the final output image.

xerography A process which places an electrostatic charge on a plate. When an image is projected onto the plate it causes the charge to dissipate in the illuminated areas. Resinous powder is applied, and adheres only to the dark, (image) areas. The powder is transferred to the paper and fused by heat.

x-height Height of body of lower-case letters, exclusive of ascenders and descenders, i.e. height of the letter x.

x-line See **mean line.**

Index